Mark Wheeller

Hard to Swallow

Adapted from the book 'Catherine'
by Maureen Dunbar

Salamander Street

PLAYS

First published 1991 by Cambridge University Press (reprinted five times between then and 1999). ISBN 0521399377

A revised edition was first published by dbda in 2000; Reprinted in January 2003 and November 2003; Further revised edition published in March 2006 and reprinted in March 2008 by Zinc Communicate ISBN 978 1 9028 4308 7

This edition first published in 2020 by Salamander Street Ltd., 272 Bath Street, Glasgow, G2 4JR (info@salamanderstreet.com)

Hard to Swallow © Mark Wheeller and Maureen Dunbar, 1991

Photograph appears with kind permission of Maureen Dunbar's family.

PB ISBN: 9781913630249
E ISBN: 9781913630256

Cover and text design by Konstantinos Vasdekis

Printed and bound in Great Britain

10 9 8 7 6 5 4 3 2 1

Further copies of this publication can be purchased from www.salamanderstreet.com

CONTENTS

Acknowledgements

Maureen Dunbar for support, guidance and advice.

John, Richard, Simon, Catherine (diaries), Anna Smith and Maureen Dunbar for permission to use their words.

Dr Tony Saunders for his medical expertise.

Sophie Gorell Barnes and MBA Literary Agents for their continued interest in my work.

Thanks to George Spender and those in the Salamander Street team for their efforts to extend the reach of my plays.

The writing team for the very first working script, then entitled *Catherine* was: Donna Batt, Martin Blackman, Sarah Blackman, Richard Brown, Paula Curtis, Jason Eames, Debbie Giles, Deanne McAteer, Kate Noss, Abigail Penny, Gary Richards, Kalwant Singh, Andrew Stott, Sharon Tanner, Chris Vaudin.

Introduction by Maureen Dunbar (2000)

My first meeting with Mark Wheeller was at the Oaklands Community School in Southampton. The reason for my visit was to decide whether or not to place my trust in him and allow him to write a play based on my book *Catherine*, the story of my daughter's fight with anorexia nervosa. No one, I thought, could convey the torment and agony of those seven years of illness.

Talking to Mark, I knew instinctively that here was a man I could say a total "Yes" to, I knew I would trust him implicitly. I could see too, how his young drama group drew inspiration from their gifted teacher.

I have followed the progress of *Hard to Swallow* from its earliest beginnings. I have never failed to be moved by the sensitive performances and also by the certain knowledge that Catherine's story has helped so many people and opened channels that did not exist before her death.

People have asked me whether I found putting pen to paper to be therapeutic – I can only say no, I did not. It was agonising. Agonising because I could see all the mistakes, the terrible mess, much more clearly in hindsight – the mistakes of doctors and my own mistakes in particular. The frustration, anger and despair that I felt many times during Catherine's illness were magnified in me as I wrote. The whole exercise was extremely painful. I wrote the book in tears.

For me the burden of grief was enormous because of the additional suffering I had caused Catherine by insisting on many occasions that she should go into hospital for treatment. When she first became ill, I had never heard of anorexia, neither had Catherine. Nobody I knew had heard of it either. During the seven long years of Catherine's illness I was always expecting doctors to come up with an answer, no one really explained what was happening to her, no one recommended books for me to read, and family counselling was never suggested. Only in writing about Catherine, after her death, did I see how wrong the treatment had been for her. How naive I had been in expecting an answer – where there was no answer. While she was alive, I was so busy trying to help, support and understand Catherine, trying to get help and treatment for her, that I was unable to stand back, try to appraise the situation and be objective.

All of these things I understood as I wrote – IN HINDSIGHT. The picture in my mind was of one huge tragic mess. The pain and grief I felt as I wrote was inexpressible. But, gradually, as I continued to put my feelings on paper, I also saw more clearly how things might have been different had I known more and also had I followed my own heart. This only added to my guilt. These thoughts and feelings, I believe, were in the deep recesses of my mind but because I had been so desperate in my search for an answer to Catherine's illness, I had never allowed them to surface – only in writing was this able to happen.

Simon, my eldest son, by encouraging me to write Catherine's story, gave me a very positive thing to do, though an extremely difficult, emotional and agonising one. Catherine's wish was that her life and death should help others. The fruits of the book have been tremendous. Many parents have written to me and said how much better they understand their children who have this frightful illness. Anorexics have told me how much more aware they are of their families' suffering. Professionals have said they have learnt what not to do. One person wrote "Catherine has disturbed the waters of our lives and made us look into the integrity of our relationships". So the book, which I initially believed could not help anyone because Catherine's was not a success story, has helped hundreds of people. Most especially, it has helped many to come to terms with their illness and removed guilt when they do not have the power to change. It has sometimes acted as a jolt to some with anorexia and aided them to start climbing the ladder to recovery.

The play *Hard to Swallow* has added in no small measure to all that is good and constructive as a result of my dear Catherine's death. My trust in Mark has been richly rewarded.

Maureen Dunbar
2000

Introduction for the original 1990 CUP publication

I hadn't heard of anorexia until I was twenty years old. My secondary school education had provided lessons about drugs, sexually transmitted diseases, how to write a curriculum vitae and fill in a tax form, but no one mentioned anorexia… in spite of the fact that one of my best friends began to stop eating in the sixth form. It went by unnoticed, or unchallenged. Teachers ignored it… no one knew anything was wrong. All we knew was Ann was becoming a lot thinner.

Some months after we'd left school and gone our separate ways, I heard from a friend that Ann had fainted on her doorstep and rushed to hospital apparently weighing about four stone. When I contacted her she was well on the road to recovery and told me her story. This was the first time I'd heard the word 'anorexia'. It meant little more to me than scurvy, i.e, a very rare illness. I never expected to hear it again.

In 1986 I was faced with the problem of a girl (Jo – we nicknamed her Jo the Unicorn as she had played a unicorn in my *King of Elfland's Daughter* musical production, so you can see where Jo the Goat comes from) seeking help from me, her teacher, as she believed she had symptoms of anorexia. Like the school I had attended as a pupil, and the school I then taught at (unlike Oaklands!), there was no literature on anorexia, though I do believe that those who opted for cookery in the upper school were given a brief warning about the dangers of dieting. Eventually we convinced this girl to visit her doctor. She was sent home with a terse:

'Well, come back in three weeks and we'll see how much you weigh.'

This was a girl who had broken her scales at home and was admitting to hiding food. It was one thing for teachers not to know about anorexia… but doctors? I was astonished.

In the course of researching for this play, I visited the local Health Education Department. They had no books on anorexia, only five or six newspaper articles and were embarrassed to admit that little was being done to promote recognition of this syndrome, despite the fact it was beginning to receive media attention.

Maureen Dunbar's book (and later the film) *Catherine* has done much to heighten public awareness of this potentially fatal syndrome. This play has continued her good work and offered increased understanding so that early preventative action can be taken. Through Patricia (and Jo the Goat!) we can see that there is hope and people can recover.

I am pleased to say that the two women who inspired my involvement in this issue are building new lives for themselves. Although they too carry a message of hope, I do believe that some of their pain could have been alleviated by a greater awareness of anorexia.

Mark Wheeller

Support and advice for anorexics and their families can be sought from:

www.beateatingdisorders.org.uk

www.eating-disorders.org.uk

Details of local contacts in your area are freely available to callers ringing the national helpline.

Introduction for the revised 2000 dbda edition

The 12 July 1989 will remain in my mind for ever. I spent the whole of the day at London's National Theatre preparing for our (Oaklands Youth Theatre) performance of *Hard to Swallow* that night, on the world-famous Olivier stage. Many of our friends and relations were there to support us. Not only that, but friends and relations of Catherine Dunbar. I realised that the feelings of pride and excitement that we were experiencing would be tempered by the fact that the play was, for them, a very real personal tragedy… a courageous exposure of the events and circumstances that led to this girl's untimely death. I reflected on Maureen's willingness to trust us with the story, but she was always quite certain that Catherine would have been keen for the play to be presented by young people.

Eighteen months previously we, at Oaklands Youth Theatre, had sat in the music room at our school discussing with Maureen the possibility of dramatising her daughter's life story so as to heighten awareness of this potentially fatal syndrome. All of us had very high hopes for the play, but none of us in our wildest dreams could have predicted that we would have the opportunity to perform it at such a prestigious venue.

There were times in the development of the play when we very nearly gave up. The more we researched, the more complex the issue seemed to become. We had to learn to trust the research material (generously given to us by Maureen) and allow it to speak for itself. Maureen, and those people whose words we have used in the play, know what they're talking about as a result of their own experience. We wanted the play to reflect that personal experience.

Our first stage of writing was literally to jigsaw puzzle the words from the research material without adding to them or altering them at all. This was done on two evenings a week by myself and a team of about ten Oaklands Youth Theatre members over a period of about three months. Our first draft, as a consequence, had very little dialogue. Most of that script was 'reported speech'.

I then took the script home and edited it. This process aimed to ensure that the play ran smoothly, wasn't too long (the first draft would have lasted nearly four hours) and had as much dialogue as possible. The resultant second draft became our rehearsal script.

I was determined that the play should be visually striking so that the style in which the play was performed became as compelling as the message the play carried. In fact, without the stylisation (which is evident from some of the scripting and in the stage directions of the Brussels sprout scene) I believe the message may have got lost in the sheer density of words. Thus, throughout rehearsals the play continued to undergo many more changes.

This new version of the play includes the developments made whilst Oaklands Youth Theatre toured the play around Texas, USA (what an amazing three weeks that was). This was after the original *Hard to Swallow* manuscript had been delivered to Cambridge University Press. It also takes into account the main way in which the play has been used since its publication; that of exam presentation and play festivals, where often the requirement is for a small cast with more or less equal opportunities.

The play has achieved repeated and considerable success in festivals.

I hope that some groups will choose to enter this play for the prestigious National Student Drama Festival as well as the All England Festival. Feel free to cut sensitively to match the time constraints of such festivals.

It must, at all times, be remembered when reading or performing this play that the events portrayed are as close to the truth as memory will allow. The performers should not impersonate the real-life characters, but breathe into them a life that is a reasonable interpretation of the words in the book. The actors should avoid overstatement and should veer towards underplaying. You can trust the material… you really can. It is after all as near as possible to the 'real thing'.

Good luck to all who choose to work with this play.

Mark Wheeller

Introduction for the 2020 Salamander Street Edition

As I sat down to start writing this introduction, I had a notification on Twitter for a "message request". The message transpired to be from Maureen's granddaughter asking me to phone her mum, Anna. I had a pretty good idea what this could be about and, sadly, I was right.

I was soon on the phone talking to Anna, who I'd briefly met at the National Theatre performance back in 1989. Maureen had passed away aged eighty-six, with her family around her. She had said what a good life she'd had. I can testify to that. Maureen's was very much a "good life" and a generous and compassionate one too.

She had given us so much by allowing us, a brand-new city Youth Theatre group from Southampton, to tell her tragic and personal story. A few years ago I wrote a resource book[1] explaining the context and development of the play. A number of the original OYT cast contributed their vivid memories and Sarah Blackman, who ended up playing Catherine, recalled her thoughts on Maureen's generosity:

As an enthusiastic teen who believed very strongly in the medium of theatre to make an impact on people's lives, it made perfect sense to me that Maureen Dunbar would allow us, an unknown entity with no track history of working together from a different socio-economic background, to be responsible for publicly portraying her story. I took her trust in our abilities for granted.

As an adult, I cannot believe she agreed! I am blown away by her braveness to do so and the risk she took. I remember her saying her belief was that people close to Catherine's age when she began to suffer from anorexia would have more of a simpatico relationship with her daughter.

Of all the information given to us for research purposes, Catherine's diaries, felt almost sacrosanct to me, verging on intrusion. I remember devouring them in one sitting, desperately trying to connect with this young woman. I was searching for clues to whatever issues in her life had led her to this "peculiar action" of strict management, and denial of food. Was her anorexia a psychological cause or a symptom?

---

[1] *Hard to Swallow – Easy To Digest* (available from Salamander Street)

We were undoubtedly affected by the material. I might even suggest that we needed to be, in order to honour it. But, come curtain down, we had the choice of how much we 'took with us' back into our real life. It is a most humbling realisation that the people we were portraying on stage did not have that choice. The most we could offer them to ameliorate their pain was to use our performance to educate, enlighten, share, engender awareness amongst others or, at the very least, elicit compassion. In this respect, I hope our ragtag group from Southampton whose play seemed to coincide with the burgeoning general awareness of anorexia nervosa at that time justified Maureen's faith in us.

Her generosity benefited us in other ways too. I remember vividly Maureen saying to us that she wanted Catherine's trust fund to grant us funds to do something exciting with the play. We decided to use these funds to initiate a project to take us (and the play) to America. Again, I shall offer Sarah's recollections (from my *Hard to Swallow – Easy To Digest* book) as they will communicate the extraordinary situation we were suddenly placed in:

I consider what happened next to represent the apex of our very own holy (theatrical) trinity:

First the Edinburgh Fringe Festival (Fringe), then the performance at the National Theatre…

… then to top it all…

… a trip to Texas! Yee hah!

Mark might as well have taken us on a tour of Mars! So alien did our contemporaries' lives seem to me then. I remember being flabbergasted by the cultural differences between two nations who spoke the same language.

We were all paired with students from The Houston School for Visual and Performing Arts, which served as our HQ. I assume every student automatically graduates with a Master's in 'dancing on the tables at lunchtime'. Everyone, and I mean everyone, was up on the nearest available surface 'bustin' moves'! It was like 'Fame'… in cowboy boots!

We participated in some of their classes which was nerve-wracking! I remember one exercise where we each had to share something we were 'afraid of'. Well, we Brits thought we'd done well by spitting out things you might expect such as 'dying', 'being alone' etc. and then one American student said;

"I'm afraid I'm going to take my dad's shotgun one of these days and kill him!"

I don't think anyone managed to top that one!

Guns, it turned out, were everywhere … including, at one school we visited, the school canteen! A change from our British dinner ladies! It was wonderfully, bizarre.

The shared enthusiasm towards theatre proved the main bonding mechanism. One friend I still have, flew to the UK and we went to the Edinburgh Festival together.

We performed in many schools and colleges over the three weeks we were there. The audiences were very receptive to our performances. They really took things to heart. The Arts students took acting very seriously. They were very interested in how we could perform something like 'Hard to Swallow' and not be negatively psychologically affected ourselves.

We performed at a hospital during the Doctors' lunchtime. They brought their sandwiches with them to the auditorium and I remember thinking "this will be interesting when it comes to the binge scene…"

I found our American cousins much more open about their feelings than we were but with an incredibly earnest overlay. Our cultural overlay is dry humour. I'd sign up for the time-machine and relive these experiences again without reservation. They were like inserting glorious technicolor onto our black and white seeming lives. It was manna from heaven for a teenager seeking heightened experiences. I don't think I slept much, there was always something to do, see, or someone to talk theatre-shop or personal ambitions with.

We also managed to impress the specialist students from HSPVA with our work:

For a young Texan just hearing a British person speak was magical. From what I remember I was blown away that y'all would have tackled a subject so "deep" back then. It was a wonderful production and inspired many of us to find more of our own voices through work that was so thought provoking and new to us.

Josh Jordan (HSPVA student 1990)

I distinctly remember that the subject was handled in such a way that teens understood it without it being "dumbed down". The imagery and staging you all used was awesome. Trying to express what was in the main character's mind. How she perceived the social world around her. Lastly, Sarah (as Catherine) was fantastic! I remember thinking "these kids are better than us." I know I was not alone in that thought.

Wade Williams (HSPVA student 1990)

These comments came as a real boost when I saw them in 2017 researching my *Easy To Digest* book. I'd always felt we had made a good impression, but for them to remember it so vividly all these years later is a further testament to the quality of my wonderful Youth Theatre performers. We were only in HSPVA for a week or two!

Just to stress her commitment to our project, Maureen came with a friend to watch one of our performances! We did all we could to thank her for giving us all these various opportunities but it's nigh on impossible to express heartfelt thanks over and over again. Maureen had given so much of herself to us and we all hoped she had gained something in return.

I went to see Maureen in 2017 at the same time as I was writing the resource book. It was wonderful to be able to inform her that *Hard to Swallow* was to become a set text for the new Eduqas GCSE (9-1) Drama exam. She was obviously delighted. No one could have anticipated that back in 1988 when we had our first contact.

As she walked me into her kitchen, I had the most wonderful surprise. There, on the side, was a picture of Catherine (the one that appeared on the front of her book) and beside it, a photo montage our Youth Theatre cast had given Maureen after the very first performance to offer her a permanent memory and show our gratitude. It was heartwarming to know that we mattered to Maureen as much as she did to us.

Speaking to Anna today was so lovely. She said how her mum always spoke warmly of the OYT years. I told her about this new publication, about which I hadn't yet said anything to Maureen. My plan was to surprise her with a copy in the post!

An incredible knock-on effect of the play becoming a set text was that I was approached by TiE It Up Theatre (who claim to "make a drama out of learning") to tour the play professionally. This had happened many years previously but schools now **need** to see the play in 3D to be able to study the play effectively. I was delighted, but also somewhat apprehensive. I knew nothing about the company nor the people behind it. They seemed nice on the phone, plus given that no one like the Royal Shakespeare Company were looking to tour it, my feeling was – nothing ventured, nothing gained.

I decided not to go and see it in their first year of touring. I had previously been in the awkward situation of having to meet the professional cast of a production of *Too Much Punch* that had been so dreadful, illustrated by the fact that the audience had laughed in the accident scene! If the first year was good enough they would get a second tour up and running and I would go and see it then. It also took pressure off them for the first tour. I offered distant support via social media as much as I could and soon saw the excellent comments from schools pouring in. Once they let me know that they were booking a second tour, I let them know I would be coming to see it.

It was a stunning production. I plan to write a fuller account in the second edition of *Hard to Swallow – Easy to Digest*, which by the time you read this will probably be out (so do have a look).

Anna, Catherine's sister, said to me she would like to see it and that is something I shall really look forward to sharing, in full confidence that she will approve of it in every way. I'm sad that Maureen never saw it. She would have loved it. So, now it offers a wonderful legacy for her work on behalf of eating disorders. Heartfelt thanks to David and Elliot at TiE It Up for their work in making the plays second chapter become such a successful one!

It's great that they have shared their story in this script on page xviii. I had no idea how much of an impact it had made on the young Elliot and am pleased that the theatricality of the play has also left its mark. That is always important for me.

The major addition to this Salamander Street edition (apart from this introduction) is the inclusion of *Crossing the Bridge – The Unseen Billy Goats Scenes*.

Since the play has become a set text it has become important for students to study the development of the play and these were a crucial part of that. I have written a detailed introduction from page 69, so I shan't elaborate here but I suggest these become a staple part of the introduction to this play.

I would offer these scenes (including the poem) to students to stage before they read the play. They will:

• explain the *raison d'être* for the Billy Goats scenes in the final version of the play more clearly than any lecture might be able to do

• introduce the animated performance style required for this form of narrative theatre that should be applied to the whole of the text

• be fun… and in a play like *Hard to Swallow*, where there are few "fun" moments, fun 'hooks' are essential

Enjoying the creative process is always crucial to any successful project regardless of the subject matter being so serious. My motto in OYT and school was always along these lines:

*Engage in Theatre for the **fun** of doing it **seriously**.*

OYT had a lot of fun doing my serious plays. We had great enjoyment from meeting the people we met along the way. One of those who we all remember particularly fondly is Maureen. I have written to those of the cast I am still in touch with, from 1999, to inform them. I know they will be sad, as am I, but they all remember Maureen for her composure, her generosity and her fervent desire to make something good out of something dreadfully bad. One of them, in her reply described her as gracious and another remembered her bringing cakes for us all… something I'm surprised I don't remember given how much I love cake!

As Anna said to me today… Mum is with Catherine now… and I know that will have been a great comfort to both her and will continue to be for her wider family.

Thank you, Maureen and may the potent impact of your words continue to be felt long after your passing.

Mark Wheeller
June 2020

A Reflection on the Touring Production by TiE It Up Theatre

Elliot Montgomery and David Chafer (TIE IT UP THEATRE) talk about their experiences of working with *Hard to Swallow*.

First Encounters with *Hard to Swallow*

For Elliot, the initial exposure to Mark Wheeller's work was during his Secondary School education, when an inspirational Drama teacher handed out a script that stirred such emotion it was to shape his entire career from that point on. That script was *Hard to Swallow*.

The play addressed the issue of eating disorders, which was unheard of at the time. The subject matter become the focus of many discussions amongst the teenage drama group for weeks and months afterwards. It moved the group to raise money to fund an on-site counsellor to support other young people but also inspired a young Elliot Montgomery to become a Drama teacher and, over thirty years later, he continues this legacy with his own Drama students. There still remains no better way to do this than by introducing young people to Mark Wheeller's plays, which all have a timeless quality and are as relevant today as when they were written. These plays take pride of place in Elliot's school drama studio, with *Hard to Swallow* as the centre-piece. Elliot introduced the text to his close friend, David Chafer, an experienced professional actor and producer, and TIE IT UP THEATRE was formed.

How was TIE IT UP THEATRE created?

It had always been an ambition of Elliot's to create a theatre company that was able to provide young people with a high quality, professional live theatre experience. David was keen to ensure that the company not only delivered an important message to young people but also provided an opportunity for talented actors to tour the UK, backed by a company with ethics and integrity at its heart. So, when Eduqas announced that *Hard to Swallow* was going to be one of their GCSE set texts for Drama it felt like an appropriate time to make that dream a reality.

<u>Rehearsing and Touring *Hard to Swallow*</u>

Mark Wheeller was (and continues to be) incredibly supportive of the company's work and they were thrilled when he gave the company permission to take the play on a national tour of UK secondary schools in the Spring of 2018. TIE IT UP THEATRE cast five incredibly talented, professional, adult actors, who were a joy to work with in rehearsals. The play was new to each of them and it was great to see how the story and its subject matter achieved the same emotionally charged reactions from them as it continues to with students across the country. This was most

evident when the cast were shown the harrowing photographs of Catherine that are used in Section 10 of the play. No matter how often we see these images they are no less shocking and we are reminded how important this play is in educating its audiences about eating disorders.

Each actor came to the first rehearsal having carried out lots of research into the story, its characters and the subject matter. Maureen Dunbar's book 'Catherine' on which the play is based, was a powerful resource that we used. In addition the company carried out extensive research into anorexia and a variety of other eating disorders.

Once the ensemble started moving from page to stage, it was important to TIE IT UP THEATRE that they created something new and didn't reinvent anything that had been done before it in its staging. It was also important that the actors felt completely comfortable in offering their ideas about how each scene could be crafted; this really was to be an open and safe rehearsal space where all ideas would be explored.

TIE IT UP THEATRE had several aims for this particular tour. Firstly, they wanted as many young people as possible to be able to see a live piece of theatre. Secondly, they wanted to help bring the text to life so that they could help Drama students with their studies. Thirdly, and most importantly, they wanted to raise awareness of the complexity of eating disorders and their impact on the families of the victims. They were constantly aware that they were performing a play about real people and they owed it to the Dunbar family to tell their story in the most truthful and sensitive way possible.

The production was created over a period of six intensive days before embarking on the two week tour. The response to the production has been overwhelming. The discussions that have taken place during the workshops afterwards have shown how many young people have been affected by eating disorders in some way. The company have received messages from teachers letting them know that some students have opened up for the first time and made a disclosure about their own battle with anorexia. They have also explored many other issues in the workshops as students have picked up on the stresses and strains that may have been caused as a result of Catherine's illness. The issue of mental health is often discussed and it is important to the company that students are signposted to where help is available for them.

TIE IT UP THEATRE have now toured the UK performing *Hard to Swallow* every Spring since 2018. To date they have performed in over seventy schools to approximately 4,500 young people.

Ann's Story[1]

Anorexia nervosa controlled my life for eleven years. Only now, at thirty, having lived free of a phobia of weight gain for four years, am I aware of how much an obsession dominated my every thought and deprived me of years of normal teenage experiences.

As a pupil at a mixed school I was certainly not the only female conscious of her figure and weight; the boys' innocent teasing was a continual reminder of my developing body – according to the lads I was curvy! However, diets became fashionable and being five foot two inches and eight stone I was not quite as slim as I would have liked to have been.

Unfortunately for me, exams coincided with my interest in losing some weight. Being amongst a group of particularly intelligent grammar school pupils, I set myself unattainably high standards and very quickly the pressures and competition associated with exams upset me. Subconsciously, my reaction to the stresses of revision was to punish my own body; my diet became stricter, and I gleaned a sense of satisfaction from the suppression of hunger. The less I ate the more in control I felt. I sat my exams weighing seven stone.

Extremely worried parents encouraged me to leave school and avoid A-Levels and further education, suggesting alternatives that would lead me away from the academic side of life. However, having achieved good O-Level results, I opted for the A-Level courses. That decision caused me two years of utter misery.

A self-imposed programme of studying and revising totally isolated me from my friends. I exaggerated the importance of high marks and in doing so, became more and more preoccupied with food, diets and weight. I read, with an insatiable urge, any article I could find, featuring slimming, until I knew from memory the calorific value of absolutely anything I consumed.

[1] The friend Mark refers to in his introduction

I kept meticulous daily records of my food intake and my weight each day. I became devious, lying to family, assuring them I had eaten at school in order to avoid joining in with everyone at conventional meal times. Home life became very tense, and rows ensued. My parents were well aware of my behaviour and regularly tried to reason with me, but as a stubborn obsessive teenager, nothing would convince me I was anything but fat.

My phobia of weight gain led to further problems. I was terribly lonely, isolating myself from social activities, one, for fear they would involve eating or drinking, and two, because I could not afford time away from my rigid study pattern. I gradually found myself without friends. No one seemed to be aware of my unhappiness. I withdrew into myself, conscious that I was different. Everyone around me seemed so carefree and vibrant, despite the fact that we were all undergoing important exams and facing major career decisions. I felt ostracised and secretly craved friendship and acceptance. Only on one occasion in two years did a friend suggest I was perhaps overdoing my diet. One teacher stopped me in the corridor and remarked I was rather thin, and another callously asked my despairing parents if they had noticed I wasn't looking too well! I began to feel trapped within a condition that had gained total control of my life.

A constant battle went on within me: on the one hand I desperately wanted to be like everyone else, but on the other I could not relinquish the power and control I exercised over my body. My inner conflict grew and exacerbated my problem. I sat my A-Levels weighing six and a half stone. Ironically, I then chose a career in hotel catering and management and embarked on an HND course at college in Cheltenham.

The first two terms at college appeared to be a turning point in my life. Lodging with a group of girls, and with no immediate exams, I began to enjoy the role of a full-time student and participated in most social events. I seemed to have unburdened myself of my obsession overnight, that is, until exams loomed once more. I was soon back on the treadmill of dieting.

Something *finally* snapped – I had slipped into a lifestyle that could not continue. I was merely existing and life itself seemed pointless. I needed to share this struggle with someone else. At last I admitted to my parents I was hopelessly trapped within a condition that was ruining my life.

I was admitted to hospital. One 'member of staff' had true control over my behaviour – the psychiatrist. He was a tall, imposing, elderly man who wielded a tremendous amount of power over staff and patients alike. An admonishment from him for behaving childishly by refusing to co-operate shamed me, on more than one occasion, into eating again. Even now, I feel he was the main reason for my recovery.

On achieving my target weight, I was released from the isolation room and given more freedom – even a visit home for the weekend. My next major hurdle was to maintain the weight.

Hospital treatment was such that, whilst a patient, whenever my weight dropped below seven stone, I was re-introduced to full-time bed rest in order to conserve energy and gain weight. Over a couple of weeks my weight stabilised and after a two-month hospital stay, I was finally in my own home for good.

Initially, coping with a new body image and weight and adjusting to normal eating patterns with family proved very hard. My weight fluctuated as did my moods. Away from controlled hospital life, the burden of sensible eating was mine once again and that pressure alone frightened and worried me. There seemed such a tenuous link between maintaining my weight and losing complete control.

My recovery was monitored with regular visits to hospital but, as I became more confident, my checks became less frequent and eventually, I was coping alone.

Years followed where I vacillated between seven and nine stone, anorexia and bulimia. With each new pressure my body was subjected to abuse – I either starved or gorged myself. However, my experience in hospital had ingrained a figure of seven stone in my mind and on every occasion that my weight dropped below it, I was pulled up short with memories of my battle with the illness whilst in hospital. On a couple of occasions I was treated as an outpatient at hospital when things became too much for me. Luckily, I knew when to ask for help. Slowly and gradually, over the next few years, I came to terms with myself and now, as a wife and mother, I am living life to the full, making up for all the years lost.

Ann, 1989

Yes, there are happy endings! Anorexia controlled my life during those precious years of growing up. Twelve years on from the above article, I remain a happily married woman with three wonderful children and free of this dreadful illness. It is merely a distant dark memory. Even during periods of stress and difficult times, such that we all encounter in our lives, when previously I would have immediately turned to controlling my weight and food, these thoughts never enter my head. I have even coped with several exams! I am living proof that this problem is curable – don't ever be afraid to ask for help.

Ann, 2000

Heading for my sixties, I am still free of something that felt like a constant ball and chain through years of my youth. I often look back and lament that I was at the mercy of an illness over which I had no control. If I were struggling now with such an awful mental health condition, I would be able to seek out the wonderful therapies on offer, such as NLP, CBT and Mindfulness, which can assist so effectively in helping someone understand the causes for this self-punishment. Being helped to understand the reasons behind your illness empowers you to think positively and start to enjoy the gift of life that you've been given.

Ann (2017)

A Note from Anna Smith (née Dunbar) (2020)

My mother, Maureen Dunbar, died of old age and dementia on 31 May 2020, surrounded by her family.

She gave seven years of her life supporting my sister Catherine, trying to show her the joys of life and instil in her the will to live and beat her illness. Sadly, Catherine died of Anorexia Nervosa in 1984.

Encouraged by my brother, Simon, Mum wrote the book *Catherine*, hoping that it would create compassion, love and support from the families and friends of those unfortunate enough to suffer Anorexia. The effect was numerous letters of support, thank yous and requests for help as well as letters from psychiatrists, psychologists, and doctors.

Mum's compassion, understanding and devotion to the eating disorder fight was hugely respected, as was she. The book, film and play had a massive impact on people's lives, as did the radio interviews and talks Mum gave. Mum's wish was to create compassion, love and support from those families and friends of those unfortunate to suffer from Anorexia, as well as create a better understanding of eating disorders.

With the success of the book and everyone's role in acting, directing and staging *Hard to Swallow*, you are all playing a key part in that message. Thank you.

At the end of her life, Mum talked about how blessed she had been in her life and how she had a wonderful family whom she loved dearly. Her final wish was for everyone to do an act of kindness each day. I now see Mum entering heaven, finally meeting Catherine again, followed by her beloved father and dear mother and her two fabulous golden retrievers bounding in to lick her face. Rest in peace.

Maureen Dunbar 1934–2020

Hard to Swallow was originally performed by the Oaklands Youth Theatre. It was premiered under the title *Catherine – The Life Story of an Anorexic* at the Edinburgh Festival Fringe in the Heriot-Watt Theatre Downstairs on 29 August 1988.

On 12 July 1989, *Hard to Swallow* was performed on the Olivier Stage at the Royal National Theatre on London's South Bank as part of the first Lloyds Bank Young Theatre Challenge. It has subsequently been performed throughout the UK, Australia, New Zealand, Canada and USA.

Characters

The play has 31 characters: 6 female, 3 male and 22 characters of either sex. Can be performed by 5 (3F & 2m) with doubling.

CATHERINE DUNBAR

JOHN DUNBAR
Catherine's father

MAUREEN DUNBAR
Catherine's mother

SIMON DUNBAR
Catherine's brother (older)

ANNA DUNBAR
Catherine's sister (younger)

NARRATOR

DADDY GOAT

MUMMY GOAT

BABY GOAT

JO THE GOAT/PATRICIA

TROLL

DR WYNNE

(CHARGE) NURSE CURTIS

NURSE BLACKMAN

PENNY

AGONY AUNT

PROFESSOR CALDERSTOW

DR CLEGG (AND OPTIONAL COLLEAGUE)

NEWS 1-3

MAUREEN 2

OBSERVERS 1 & 2

POLICE 1 & 2

DIARY 1-3

CHOIR BOY/GIRL

Hard to Swallow has often been performed by an all-female cast.

With careful doubling *Hard to Swallow* can be performed by five actors:

FEMALE 1
Baby, Catherine

FEMALE 2
Mummy, Maureen

FEMALE 3
Jo, Anna, News 1, Dr Wynne, Nurse Blackman,
Samantha Double Yellow Line, Maureen 2, Diary
1, Patricia, Miscellaneous props!

MALE 1
Daddy, John, News 2, Dr Clegg, Observer 1, Police
1,
Diary 2, Miscellaneous props!

MALE 2
Narrator, Troll, Simon, News 3, Charge Nurse Curtis,
Penny, Psychotherapist, Observer 2, Police 2, Diary 3,
Miscellaneous props!

Try to play this scene in as animated and stylistic manner as possible. Some of the best versions I have seen have had four actors multi rolling. This has forced them to be imaginative about, for example, the creation of the Troll. This grotesque creature can be been created by all the performers suddenly becoming this one character[1] and swiftly returning to become their original roles. There are also possibilities to re-visit this creature to enable the audience to see the Drs through Catherine's eyes later in the play (Section 6).

Aim for cartoon/comedy style differentiation in the portrayal of the family of goats. Use every possibility to make this scene both engaging and funny. Adding the occasional involuntary "Bah" always goes down well. Feel free to play with the scene! It needs to be a highlight!

---

[1] For an example of how to do this see the Billy Goat 4 play on the bonus feature *Crossing The Bridge* (by RSCoYT) on the *Hard to Swallow* DVD/ download available from Salamander Street.

Section 1

THE BILLY GOATS

NARRATOR: Once upon a time there was a family of goats.

DADDY: There was a daddy goat.

MUMMY: There was a mummy goat.

BABY: And a baby goat.

ALL: Aaah!

MUMMY & DADDY: High expectations.

MUMMY: To cross the bridge.

DADDY: To live in the green field.

MUMMY & DADDY: Just like we did when we were young.

MUMMY & DADDY: Cross the bridge.

BABY: But I must tidy my playpen.

MUMMY & DADDY: Cross the bridge.

BABY: Tidy my playpen.

MUMMY, DADDY & NARRATOR: *(Chanting)* Cross the bridge… cross the bridge… cross the bridge… cross the bridge…

TROLL: *(Leaping onto the bridge blocking **BABY**'s path. Threatening.)* Troll!

BABY: Scared.

TROLL: *(Threatening.)* Troll!

BABY: Scared. *(Running to parents.)*

TROLL: *(Threatening.)* Troll!

MUMMY: Protection.

BABY: Safety.

DADDY: Seethe.

BABY: Playpen. *(Goes into it.)* Security.

DADDY: Open the door!

MUMMY: Leave Baby alone…

DADDY: Cross the bridge!

MUMMY: Be patient.

DADDY: Open the door.

MUMMY: Leave Baby alone.

DADDY: Cross the bridge!

MUMMY: Be patient.

DADDY: *(To* **MUMMY***.)* Don't you see? Baby will never come out!

NARRATOR: Visitor from a neighbouring field.

JO: Jo the Goat. *(To* **MUMMY***.)* Playpen.

MUMMY: Cross the bridge.

JO: Playpen… just like Baby's.

MUMMY: Here it is… but our baby never came out.

TROLL: You can have one too. I'll build one for you…

JO: Small… Frightening…

TROLL: You can have one too. I'll build one for you.

JO: I don't like it… I don't want it.

MUMMY, DADDY & NARRATOR: Cross the bridge… cross the bridge… cross the bridge…

TROLL: *(Disheartened.)* You can have one too. I'll build one for you.

    TROLL *sits on the bridge sobbing as* **JO** *successfully crosses the bridge.*

MUMMY, DADDY & NARRATOR: Cross**ed** the bridge.

    (Silence.)

Section 2

CHRISTMAS '73 – THE DUNBAR HOUSEHOLD

MAUREEN, **JOHN**, **SIMON**, **ANNA** and **CATHERINE** *are seated round their dining table. In 'fast forward' motion they mime eating their Christmas dinner etc. The family are enjoying themselves, pulling crackers etc. accompanied by Christmas Carol which is also sped up. Each of the characters wears a party hat for the duration of this scene. The aim of the scene is to illustrate a happy family.*

ALL: Christmas 1973.

MAUREEN & JOHN: Christmas Day. Five o'clock in the morning.

SIMON: Wakey wakey!

ANNA, SIMON & CATHERINE: Celebration!

ANNA: Bleary eyes focus on.

ANNA, SIMON & CATHERINE: *(Screaming with excitement.)* Christmas stockings… rush.

CATHERINE: Lots of new toys.

ANNA, SIMON & CATHERINE: Loads of noise!

ANNA: Sweets.

ANNA, SIMON & CATHERINE: Lots to eat. Mmmm! Tasty!

SIMON: Ten-fifteen.

ANNA, SIMON & CATHERINE: *(Sung a la plainsong.)* Time for church.

ANNA: Anna… brand-new blouse.

SIMON: Simon… brand-new tie.

ANNA & CATHERINE: *(Jokingly.)* Sexy!

CATHERINE: Catherine… a brand-new skirt.

ANNA, SIMON & CATHERINE: Ready.

JOHN: Christmas, and the weeks leading up to it, were always a time of activity, excitement and joyfulness in our family. We always paid a visit to…

ANNA, SIMON & CATHERINE: Harrods' toy department. Wow!

JOHN: And nearer Christmas we would make another trip to London to see the lights and the giant Christmas tree in Trafalgar Square.

ANNA, SIMON & CATHERINE: Spectacular!

MAUREEN: Catherine always had a deep and abiding faith in God, and despite all the modern trappings never once forgot the true reason for celebrating Christmas; the cards which she made herself always reflected this.

JOHN: We were at this time, in my opinion, an ideal family. Financially we were moving ahead rapidly and I had an excellent career with a good income and benefits.

MAUREEN: This was the first Christmas for us in our beautiful new house.

JOHN: It was idyllic. It was in lovely surroundings and had a swimming pool and a tennis court. Unfortunately though, we had not been able to sell our previous house so we had to take out a very heavy bridging loan.

MAUREEN: Our euphoria about the new house was very short lived.

JOHN: The world economy collapsed.

NEWS 1: Arab-Israeli War – Oil Prices Soar.

NEWS 2: British Miners' Strike.

NEWS 3: Three-Day Working Week.

NEWS 1: Government forced into…

ALL: General election.

JOHN: Property prices slumped, interest rates rose and we came near to bankruptcy. Catherine's anorexia was, I believe, sparked off by our situation as a result of this crisis. Refusing to eat was the easiest way for her to protest, because for her eating had never been a great pleasure.

MAUREEN: Kate, as we then called her, had always been a difficult eater. I suppose the problem started when she was eight weeks old and I was forced into bottle feeding her because my milk supply had dried up.

I tried everything but nothing suited her.

After a week or so her abdomen became hard and swollen and she was obviously in pain. I was advised to cut out all milk from her diet. I gave her Ribena and Farex mixed with water and it seemed to do the trick.

JOHN: As a young child Kate was fussy about her eating.

MAUREEN: For years her diet consisted of bread, butter, peanut butter, cheese, yoghurt, fruit, sausages and the occasional rasher of bacon. Remembering the miseries I had endured as a child of being forced to eat what I didn't want I never forced Kate. She was never ill so was obviously getting the right nutriments. However, her attitude towards food infuriated John.

JOHN: My early years were spent with my grandparents in Liverpool at the time of food scarcity during the Second World War. I believed that she should eat what was prepared for her… and be thankful for it!

MAUREEN: Frequently, I removed her plate when John wasn't looking, purely to avoid a scene. Kate was a confident, happy little girl with common sense far beyond her years. I didn't want John's Victorian attitudes and authoritarianism to interfere with her development.

JOHN: I thought she was a very obstinate and rather strong-willed little girl.

CATHERINE: Is everybody listening? There's something I'd like to say to you all. I've decided that from now on you are all to call me Catherine. That is my baptismal name and I shall no longer answer to Kate.

JOHN: And why have we decided this, young Madam?

CATHERINE: 'Kate' is too childish.

SIMON: *(Sarcastically.)* Right! No one can call me Simon from now on. You'll all have to call me Simeus Maximus Superbus!

CATHERINE: I'm being perfectly serious. I won't talk to any of you unless you call me Catherine.

JOHN: Does it really matter?

CATHERINE: *(Agitated.)* Yes, it does. It's a simple request. If you do what I say there won't be any problem.

JOHN: Calm yourself down or I'll be raising my voice.

CATHERINE: So long as everyone understands.

MAUREEN: Within a few weeks she had us all trained and from then on she was known to everyone as Catherine.

JOHN: This stubbornness did, however, breed a determination to do well in almost everything that she tackled, be it schoolwork, sport, ballet or drama.

MAUREEN: She was a perfectionist… working unceasingly… even obsessively.

JOHN: However, she never showed any signs of excess weight and it was never, as far as I can remember, discussed.

MAUREEN: Just before Catherine returned to school in the summer of 1975 she developed severe digestive problems with a hard, slightly swollen abdomen, just as when she was a tiny baby. We cut out all milk products but it didn't do any good so we took her to our doctor.

DR WYNNE: I'm afraid that there isn't really very much that we can do for her, Mrs Dunbar.

MAUREEN: What do you mean?

DR WYNNE: You said yourself… she's a very sensitive girl.

MAUREEN: I don't understand.

DR WYNNE: This condition is often brought about by anxiety.

MAUREEN: Anxiety?

DR WYNNE: You say that you were having to sell your house?

MAUREEN: Yes?

DR WYNNE: How does Catherine feel about that?

MAUREEN: Very upset.

DR WYNNE: Maybe… when you finally move she'll be fine again.

MAUREEN: I don't think so.

DR WYNNE: Why do you say that?

MAUREEN: It's all so complicated.

DR WYNNE: Catherine probably feels this as well… you've got to talk to her about it.

MAUREEN: I do… I do… it's… it's just that John… we're moving to a small flat in London… Catherine can't bear it. We can't take our dog with us. She's devastated about it all.

DR WYNNE: And your husband?

MAUREEN: He feels as though he's failed us all.

DR WYNNE: I see.

MAUREEN: Actually, he's in a desperate state… you don't want to hear all of this.

DR WYNNE: No, it's important… please.

MAUREEN: *(Pause.)* He may lose his job… he's fighting it… but… he's under such pressure. The children are away at school during the week but of course they're there at the weekends. Catherine seems to be taking it worse than the others… and that sets John off…

DR WYNNE: What do you mean?

MAUREEN: He's begun to… well, in my view, he drinks more than perhaps he ought to.

DR WYNNE: Do you think he'd be prepared to come in and see me?

MAUREEN: I wish he would but…

DR WYNNE: You could say…

MAUREEN: There's no point, it'd cause a row. To be really honest, Doctor, there are times when even I am frightened of him.

DR WYNNE: And Catherine?

MAUREEN: Her being upset makes him even worse…
(To audience.)
Dr Wynne suggested we gave Catherine plenty of roughage to try and slow down her digestive system. This we did, and, although she continued to do well academically, she appeared pale, tired and emotionally withdrawn.

Five weeks into the Spring term something happened which marked my realisation that something was seriously wrong with Catherine. Sadly for Simon it happened on a day which, for him, should have been a day to celebrate.

MAUREEN & SIMON: Post!

SIMON: Brilliant news!

MAUREEN: What?

SIMON: First choice medical school.

MAUREEN: Simon!

SIMON: Amazing, Mum!

MAUREEN: Wonderful!

SIMON: Relief!

MAUREEN: Phone Dad!

SIMON: What, now?

MAUREEN: Yeh, now!

SIMON: Wasn't that him on the phone a minute ago?

MAUREEN: No.

SIMON: I thought… but you were talking about Catherine.

MAUREEN: It was Catherine's headmistress. They're sending her home from school.

SIMON: What?

MAUREEN: I have to meet her at the station at midday.

SIMON: What on earth's she done?

MAUREEN: They tell me that she hasn't eaten anything at all for the last two weeks. They're sending Anna home with her because they're not sure that she'll cope on her own.

SIMON: Surely if it was really serious she'd have come home with a teacher.

MAUREEN: I suppose so… anyway we should be celebrating your success. I'll go and pour you a drink. You go and phone Dad.

SIMON: Do you want to have a word with him… about Catherine.

MAUREEN: *(Pause.)* No. I want him to enjoy your news.

SIMON: When Catherine arrived home I… well, I hardly recognised her.

MAUREEN: The shock I felt at seeing her is as vivid today as it was then.

SIMON: Quite seriously, I thought that she was a friend of Anna's that I didn't know!

MAUREEN: She was pale, drawn, hollow-eyed and only able to walk very slowly.

CATHERINE enters with her face painted white (or she administers white paint to her own face as she enters) to symbolise her 'difference'. OYT used the first part of 'Innocence and Guilt' by Steve Harley and Cockney Rebel to underscore her entrance. She walks in a robotic (doll-like) style which returns to a naturalistic style as soon as she speaks.

Section 3

REFUSING TO EAT

CATHERINE: Mummy, I can't swallow. Mummy, I'm really frightened!

MAUREEN: You're at home now. We'll soon get you better. I've made some pasta, I know you like that.

CATHERINE: I'll only eat if I can eat on my own in the kitchen. I don't want Daddy to see me eating!

JOHN: I've never heard anything so ridiculous in all my life. If she's going to eat then she'll eat with us at our table!

CATHERINE: I'm not eating in front of him!

JOHN: You know the rules. You'll eat when and where you're told to. If you don't you'll be punished!

CATHERINE: You can't make me eat!

JOHN: We'll soon see about that.
(He grabs her and makes her sit.)

MAUREEN: John, she's not well.

JOHN: I insist she eats with us.

CATHERINE: I ate something about an hour ago! I'm not hungry!

JOHN: Stop being so stubborn, all I'm asking is that you eat.

CATHERINE: Just leave me alone!

JOHN: What did you say? *(**CATHERINE** is crying.)* How dare you speak to me like that!

CATHERINE: Please, Daddy! Please don't force me!

JOHN: You will do as you are told. You will eat!
*(**CATHERINE** storms out.)* Catherine!

MAUREEN: Leave her, John. It'll only make matters worse.

JOHN: Why do you always do that?

MAUREEN: Do what?

JOHN: Take her side. Can't you see if she goes on getting her own way things will get even worse?

(**JOHN** *goes to exit as if to retrieve* **CATHERINE.**)

MAUREEN: You don't understand! The school have sent her home because they think that she hasn't eaten anything for nearly two weeks.

JOHN: *(Incredulous.)* Two weeks?

MAUREEN: That's what the school have told me.

JOHN: And what does Catherine have to say?

MAUREEN: She says it hurts when she swallows.

JOHN: Why didn't you tell me?

MAUREEN: I was going to… later on.

JOHN: Well, we'd better do something about it.

MAUREEN: The school have advised me to contact a psychiatrist.

JOHN: A psychiatrist?

MAUREEN: Catherine needs help.

JOHN: Not that kind!

MAUREEN: She thinks she's fat.

JOHN: She's not!

MAUREEN: But she thinks she is.

JOHN: How can she be fat if she hasn't eaten for two weeks? It doesn't make sense.

MAUREEN: That's why she needs to see a psychiatrist.

JOHN: She needs to be sat down at our table and made to eat.

MAUREEN: She's agreed to eat… so long as we allow her to eat on her own. Does it really matter where she eats?

JOHN: Yes it does! Of course it does!

MAUREEN: As far as I'm concerned she can eat every meal alone, so long as she does eat!

JOHN: She will eat with us in our dining room and there will be no more arguments!

MAUREEN: It's not as simple as that.

JOHN: It is! Simon and Anna eat with us so why can't Catherine? We will not pander to her.

MAUREEN: John, please… trust me… just this once.

(Silence.)

JOHN: Maureen, I am the head of this family and therefore I am the one who makes decisions.

MAUREEN: Be it on your own head.

(Pause.)

Even when he dragged her back to the table she would secretly place her food in her pockets and little, if any, was ever consumed.

One week later she was admitted to hospital having lost more and more weight every day.

Section 4

FIRST ADMISSION TO HOSPITAL

Throughout the opening part of this scene **CATHERINE** *is seated with* **NURSE BLACKMAN,** *away from* **MAUREEN** *and* **NURSE CURTIS**. *She murmurs "Mummy don't leave me" repeatedly.* **NURSE BLACKMAN** *comforts her.*

MAUREEN: What's going to happen to her?

NURSE CURTIS: *(To* **MAUREEN**.) At meal times she will start off on single portions, and then increase to double portions. Catherine's normal weight has been established as eight stone and this is to be her 'target' weight. It will be achieved by a 'privilege' regime.

MAUREEN: What do you mean by that?

NURSE CURTIS: Well, as her weight increases she'll be allowed various privileges such as being allowed to go to the bathroom instead of using a bedpan, walking around the ward rather than being confined to her bed, wearing her own clothes, receiving letters and having visitors. On the other hand if weight is lost her privileges will be denied.

CATHERINE: Mummy, don't let them put me in here.

MAUREEN: This all sounds rather cruel.

CATHERINE: I'm not a criminal. I don't need to be locked up.

NURSE CURTIS: She will be in expert hands, Mrs Dunbar. Now, I think it would be best for you to leave with a minimum of fuss.

CATHERINE: Mummy, take me home. Take me home, Mummy!

MAUREEN: I'd like to say goodbye to her before I leave.

NURSE CURTIS: Of course Mrs Dunbar… but make it as brief as possible… for Catherine's sake.

They move towards **CATHERINE**. **MAUREEN** *stoops down to her.*

MAUREEN: Catherine, I've come to say goodbye.

CATHERINE: Don't let them do this to me, Mummy!

MAUREEN: You'll have nothing to worry about.

CATHERINE: Don't leave me in here with these people. They're all mad, Mummy. I'm not mad. Don't leave me!

MAUREEN: I've talked to the nurse and you're in very good hands… Catherine, we're doing this for you.

CATHERINE: This isn't for me! I want to go home!

MAUREEN: I've got to go now, Catherine… Goodbye, Catherine.

CATHERINE: *(Breaking free from* **NURSE BLACKMAN**, *she runs towards* **MAUREEN** *and grasps her tightly.)* Mummy, you can't let them do this to me. Mummy, take me home. Mummy! No, Mummy! *(Screaming frantically.)* Mummy, Mummy, you can't leave me here with all these weird people. I'm not mad, Mummy… I'm not mad! Mummy, Mummy.

> **CATHERINE** *clings to* **MAUREEN** *screaming.* **NURSES** *drag her back and guide* **MAUREEN** *off.* **CATHERINE** *breaks down and her sobbing underscores* **PENNY**'s *speech.*

PENNY: *Just Seventeen.* The problem page. Page 32…

Dear Samantha, I'm fat. I'm fifteen and I weigh ten stone. I've talked to my mum but she says I can lose weight when I'm older and won't allow me to diet. She says it's dangerous. I get very depressed and angry about my weight, and no one understands how I feel.

SAMANTHA: Dear Penny, diets can be dangerous if they're not carried out sensibly; but being overweight, worrying about it, and hating yourself is dangerous too. If you're serious about losing weight then the first thing to do is to talk to your own doctor, explain your feelings and ask for help. A diet under medical supervision would not be dangerous, and if you lost weight sensibly you'd feel a lot happier.

CATHERINE: I've never heard of anorexia… What is it?

NURSE CURTIS: It's what you've been going through for the past few months – this obsession with losing weight. Catherine, you've denied yourself food for an unusually long time. It's dangerous. People do die from anorexia.

ANNA: I remember visiting Catherine in hospital. She had put on weight and looked very bloated. Mummy emphasised that I should not comment on how she looked. We were going out for a meal afterwards; Catherine said how much she would like to come. 'What a relief,' I thought, 'Catherine's better!'

MAUREEN: Anna, we've got some good news. The doctors have said that Catherine is ready to come home tomorrow.

ANNA: I knew she'd get better, Mummy, I knew she would.

MAUREEN: There is something else, Anna.

ANNA: What's that?

MAUREEN: I'm afraid… Daddy has lost his job.

ANNA: Are we going to have to move again… Catherine'll hate that.

MAUREEN: No. Daddy is going to be working in Saudi Arabia. He'll be leaving in a couple of weeks. It's going to be you, me and Simon looking after Catherine for the next few months, or maybe even years.

CATHERINE: *(All the diary entries could be accompanied by the musical box music to create an other-worldly atmosphere. OYT used the extract from the song referred to earlier.)*

10 March 1978:

I feel fed up and depressed with life.

Sometimes I feel like committing suicide. It is my faith in God that stops me from doing it. He gave me life and it would be the Devil who would make me take it away.

I wish I didn't feel like this. I'd give anything in the world to be a natural sane girl but it doesn't seem meant for me yet.

I am obsessed with my weight. How can I overcome it? It is an impossible task all alone.

Section 5

AT THE MEAL TABLE

MAUREEN: Stay there a moment you two. I'm determined to see that Catherine eats something this lunch time.

SIMON: Mum, what are you going to do?

MAUREEN: Auntie Eileen thinks Catherine will listen to me. She's suggested that I try to force Catherine to eat.
(To **CATHERINE***, who is in her room.)* Catherine, dinner's ready!

CATHERINE: I've already eaten.

MAUREEN: You've got to come and eat with us. I've cooked one of your favourites.

CATHERINE: What's it?

MAUREEN: Spaghetti Bolognese.

CATHERINE: I don't want it!

MAUREEN: Catherine. Come down now… please. I want you to sit at our table and eat with us.

Long silence. **MAUREEN** *waits. Finally* **CATHERINE** *crosses to the table and sits. They eat their meal in a stylistic, almost robotic manner with* **CATHERINE** *tapping her knife/fork on her plate in a rhythmic manner.*

MAUREEN: Eat.

SIMON: Enjoy.

ANNA: Swallow.

CATHERINE: Play.

ALL except CATHERINE: Finished!

ANNA: Mummy, I've finished. May I leave the table?

MAUREEN: Yes, Anna, of course you can.

SIMON: Thanks, Mum… really nice. Can I leave the table? I want to give Jenny a ring.

MAUREEN: Yes, but don't be on too long.

CATHERINE: Mummy, may I leave the table please?

MAUREEN: No, Catherine. You haven't finished.

CATHERINE: It's too cold.

MAUREEN: I'll heat it up for you if you like.

CATHERINE: It didn't taste like normal. What had you put in the sauce?

MAUREEN: It's exactly as I normally make it.

CATHERINE: Well in that case I obviously don't like spaghetti bolognese anymore.

MAUREEN: I thought it was your favourite.

CATHERINE: If you make me eat this… I'll hate you.

MAUREEN: Come on, Catherine, don't be so obstinate! What do you think would happen to you if you gave up eating altogether?

CATHERINE: I'd probably die, and then I wouldn't be such a burden to you all.

MAUREEN: I don't intend on letting you do that. Come on, darling… have at least one mouthful.
(She tries to feed **CATHERINE***.)*

CATHERINE: *(Frantically pushing the fork away.)* I can't. You know I can't swallow it. Mummy, why are you of all people being like this.
(She tips up plate in frustration and leaves.)

SIMON: *(Entering.)* What's happened?

MAUREEN: It's all my fault.

SIMON: It's not, Mum.

MAUREEN: I just couldn't see it through.

SIMON: You mustn't blame yourself.

MAUREEN: If she goes on like this she will end up killing herself.
(Pause.)

They're trying to get me to sign for her to be put in a psychiatric hospital.

She's become absolutely addicted to laxatives.

SIMON: Laxatives?

MAUREEN: She takes about a hundred every day.

SIMON: A hundred laxatives?

MAUREEN: I'm going to have to sign the forms… but I really don't want to! She'll never forgive me!

CATHERINE: *(At her table. Musical box music in background.)*

29 March 1978:

I have done so much damage to myself with three overdoses of laxatives in three weeks. I am, thank God, 6 stone 8 at the moment and intend on staying like that. I am depressed and I want to hide from people, from uncertainty, and from life itself. I feel like a rag doll which has lost its stuffing.

Section 6

IN AND OUT OF HOSPITAL

In the presentation the robotic movement style could be used to emphasise the stylistic presentation and thus emphasise the mechanical repetition of the ritual feeding.
The presentation of **DR CLEGG** *could be as though through* **CATHERINE'***s eyes, as a grotesque monster (echo of the Troll from the opening section) forcing her to do something she doesn't want to do. If you have the flexibility of casting, do have two (or more) Doctors to play this role speaking chorally.*

DR CLEGG: Psychiatric hospital admission – Catherine Dunbar. Aged sixteen.

CATHERINE: I will eat.

DR CLEGG: Feed… feed.

CATHERINE: Bloated.

MAUREEN: *(To* **ANNA***.)* Now, don't comment on Catherine's appearance.

DR CLEGG: Discharged.

ANNA: Catherine. It's lovely to see you!

CATHERINE: I won't eat.

ANNA: Please.

CATHERINE: No.

ANNA: Please.

CATHERINE: No.

ANNA: Please.

CATHERINE: No.

MAUREEN: Leave her, Anna.

DR CLEGG: Hospital re-admission – Catherine Dunbar. Aged seventeen.

CATHERINE: I will eat.

DR CLEGG: Feed… feed.

CATHERINE: Bloated.

MAUREEN: *(To* **ANNA***.)* Now, don't comment on Catherine's appearance.

DR CLEGG: Discharged.

ANNA: Catherine. It's lovely to see you!

CATHERINE: I won't eat.

ANNA: Please.

CATHERINE: No.

ANNA: Please.

CATHERINE: No.

ANNA: Please.

CATHERINE: No.

MAUREEN: Leave her, Anna.

DR CLEGG: Hospital re-admission – Catherine Dunbar. Aged eighteen.

CATHERINE: I will eat.

DR CLEGG: Feed… feed.

MAUREEN: *(Interrupting.)* Stop! This isn't working! Isn't there anything else?

PROF. CALDERSTOW: *(Entering a la superhero.)* Enter psychotherapist.

DR CLEGG: Interference.

MAUREEN & ANNA: Hope.

CATHERINE: I'll give it a try.

PROF. CALDERSTOW: Question.

CATHERINE: Answer.

PROF. CALDERSTOW: Deeper.

CATHERINE: Deeper.

PROF. CALDERSTOW & MAUREEN: Phone call.

ANNA & MAUREEN: A holiday? In Saudi Arabia? Yes, John. That would be lovely.

MAUREEN: No… Catherine's fine… she's seeing a psychotherapist.

ANNA & MAUREEN: At last! *(They exit.)* Saudi Arabia here we come!

PROF. CALDERSTOW: Come to America? Series of lectures? Yes, Sir! That would be lovely! *(S/he exits.)*

DR CLEGG: Hospital re-admission. Catherine Dunbar. Aged eighteen.

CATHERINE: I will eat.

DR CLEGG: Feed… feed.

CATHERINE: Bloated.

DR CLEGG: Ready for discharge on mother's return.

CATHERINE: Great.

MAUREEN: Return to England.

DR CLEGG: No, Mrs Dunbar. I'm afraid that Catherine has not been receiving psychotherapy.

MAUREEN: But when I left Professor Calderstow assured me that she would.

DR CLEGG: Ah… well… I'm afraid Professor Calderstow was called out to America at very short notice.

MAUREEN: This is unforgivable. My daughter is seriously ill and needed treatment. I left here confident in the knowledge that Catherine was receiving psychotherapy. So often before, you doctors have dealt with the weight problem, leaving aside the real psychological problems. She eats to escape from hospital, to return home and starve herself. I really believed that this time, with the help of psychotherapy, we would break it.
What you have failed to do for my daughter is appalling! I can't believe you've allowed it to happen!

DR CLEGG: Obviously we apologise, Mrs Dunbar. Perhaps we can offer Catherine a course of psychotherapy in the coming weeks.

MAUREEN: *(To audience.)* In September 1980 she was discharged and embarked on a secretarial course. Her weight was back to normal but she felt ugly and bloated.

VOICE 1: Catherine! You've been awarded a diploma!

ALL: *(Chorally thrusting arms in the air in celebration.)* Yeh!

VOICE 2: Catherine! You've got a job!

ALL: Yeh!

VOICE 3: Catherine! You've passed your driving test!

ALL: Yeh!

VOICE 4: Catherine…

(Silence.)

ALL: Would you like to come out for a meal?

Silence. All freeze looking at **CATHERINE** *who looks away slowly.*

MAUREEN: She would spend days in dread at being asked to the fortnightly meals the other girls at the dentist surgery tried to organise. She'd feel guilty at refusing the invitation. She worried that the others would consider her unfriendly and aloof.

Section 7

A FAMILY DIVISION

Each of the characters move, or ideally are moved, like puppets, into an appropriate freeze frame to create highly stylised presentation, physically illustrating the family dynamics and how they alter. If the Dunbar family are being used as puppets, the spoken lines should be taken by their respective puppeteers.

JOHN: Catherine's father eventually abandoned Saudi Arabia. Life there had become a nightmare for him.

MAUREEN: After a few uneasy weeks at home Maureen decided she needed to go away.

JOHN: John was left alone with Catherine and the burden of her illness.

CATHERINE: And perhaps, in this time, John became closer to Catherine than he had ever been.

MAUREEN: Maureen felt it was her duty to return to the family, and did so after about three months. She was very unhappy and unable to settle to anything.

MAUREEN & JOHN: Catherine placed great dependence on her mother and needed all the love and patience she could provide.

CATHERINE: *(Musical box music fades up.)* 14 January 1980.

MAUREEN: Catherine was now eighteen years old.

CATHERINE: I feel too thin. I want to be able to wear nice clothes again. I know that I will feel better and more normal in every sense if I can put on some more weight. I long to feel as a girl of my age should feel.

Section 8

THE BRUSSELS SPROUTS SCENE

The whole of this scene is performed stylistically with people frantically changing roles, playing scenery, properties and characters. The energy of the supporting cast must create a pacey atmosphere illustrating **MAUREEN***'s internal panic. The choreography of the changing body-props should be such that* **MAUREEN***'s lines can be spoken at life-rate speed. The changing of the props should not slow the spoken word down at all!*

MAUREEN *herself should be rushing around and, as the scene continues, becoming more out of breath with the effort to achieve her task on time.*

The contrast in pace immediately following the lines "… successful in my quest…" and "I hate you" should provide dramatic "moments" highlighting the manner in which **MAUREEN** *feels she has been let down by, or has let down her daughter.*

Throughout the scene **CATHERINE** *should be staged doing a repetitive action such as laying and re-laying the table, or brushing her hair. She begins the scene doing this action slowly and calmly (although obsessively), gradually becoming more frustrated, leading finally to her angry outburst on her line "Mummy, you're late!"*

MAUREEN: Catherine's life was regulated by a strict routine and if it was broken, by however small a margin, she would panic and cry. There was a period, for example, when she would only eat frozen Brussels sprouts… and on one day when I had been especially busy, I'd forgotten to buy Catherine these blessed Brussels sprouts. I looked in the freezer…

(Everyone becomes a 'showbiz!' freezer which opens dramatically [dance school style] at the appropriate moment. They could shout "Freezer" or shiver briefly for comic or enlivening effect.)

…but there were none there, so I dashed out to the car…

(Cast make a car with features such as windscreen wipers, etc.)

and went to Sainsbury's in the town…

I'd thought I might park on the double yellow line…

(Some break off the car to represent the double yellow line and perhaps wave to the audience.)

OBSERVERS 1 & 2: Oh… double yellow line!

MAUREEN: And rush into Sainsbury's to get them, to avoid any scenes with Catherine. But, to my dismay, the police were parked opposite.

Two more cast members break away from the car to become the **POLICE**.

POLICE 1 & 2: 'Ello, 'ello, 'ello!

MAUREEN: I could hardly imagine how I could explain to them, my urgent need for frozen Brussels sprouts.

MAUREEN 2: *(Running to the police as though desperate and worn out.)*
I've just got to get some frozen Brussels sprouts for my daughter! *(This could alternatively be spoken by the whole of the 'chorus' who turn to Maureen appealing in desperation.*
The **POLICE** *look at one another in sheer disbelief… [opportunity for brief comedy double take?])*

MAUREEN: So… much to my annoyance, I drove on to the hypermarket some three miles away, which had its own car park. I dashed in…
(Speeding through some cast-made 'automatic doors'… preferably the rotating variety to add more involvement.)
… bought the frozen Brussels sprouts…
(Speedily through the cast-made 'check-out' and till person. The key word here is speedily… as immediately **MAUREEN** *has said the five words above, the till morphs back into the car. There is a temptation to hang around here and show off the till but it needs to be made for a moment only to maintain the pace.)*
And drove back, arriving home in a panic, but relieved to have been successful in my quest…
(Two of the cast break off from the car to make an arched door frame for **CATHERINE** *to emerge from.)* …only to be greeted by a very distraught Catherine on the doorstep.

CATHERINE: *(Beside herself with rage.)* Mummy! You're late!

At this point the supporting cast should very slowly and smoothly put their hands to their heads and move in slow motion to a foetal position on the floor, representing the repressed internal agony **MAUREEN** *experiences as this argument occurs… the supporting cast's journey to the foetal position should be concluded at precisely the same time as* **CATHERINE** *exits.*

MAUREEN: Catherine… it's only five past one!

CATHERINE: *(Raging.)* That's not the point! Lunch is at one! I didn't know where you were. I couldn't find my lunch… I shall never eat a Brussels sprout again!

MAUREEN: But Catherine, I've just been out… purely to buy them.

CATHERINE: *(Raging.)* It's too late now! You know I always eat at one o'clock. You've ruined my whole day now! I hate you when you do this to me! I hate you!

The supporting cast should be immediately silent and motionless. **CATHERINE** *exits in a mood.* **MAUREEN** *looks on. There is a pause as* **MAUREEN** *turns, in slow motion, to face the audience… there is silence as she takes a deep breath to help her regain her composure.*

MAUREEN: And I was feeling so pleased with myself for having gone to all that trouble.

Section 9

BINGEING

This is one of the few scenes to benefit from naturalistic staging. During the following three speeches the cast should deliver a wide variety of food to **CATHERINE***, placed carefully on a tablecloth. It should contain savoury and sweet in separate dishes.*

During the binge, which begins as the diaries are reported, **CATHERINE** *will begin eating with her hands selecting dishes carefully. Gradually she will become more frenetic. Her face will become messy and food may well drip down her clothes. In past performances, a dollop of tomato sauce on something sweet prior to being eaten has proved an effective way of horrifying the audience!* [2]

MAUREEN: Catherine hardly ever swallowed solid food. The only time she did was during a binge. At all other times she would chew the food, then remove it from her mouth and place it in a basin. Should she be eating anywhere outside her home, then the basin was replaced by a secret plastic bag, or sometimes her pockets.

(The musical box music fades in and remains audible throughout this section fading on the last line.)

CATHERINE: Bingeing is the only way I have of remaining in my own world. It takes my mind off everything. Vomiting uses my mental and physical energies. Sometimes it leaves me hyperactive but tonight it left me drowsy.

MAUREEN: For about a year Catherine kept a record of all the food she prepared for herself.

(As the following lines are spoken **CATHERINE** *binges.)*

DIARY 1: 29 June 1981:

Mood: Fair

Weight: 4 stone 10 pounds

Breakfast: Tea, Kit-Kat

---

[2]   Sarah, who played Catherine on the original OYT production, talks extensively about her approach to this scene in the resource book *Hard to Swallow – Easy To Digest* available from Salamander Street.

DIARY 2: Lunch:

Tea, soda water, Kit-Kat, 2 Cinnamon Danish, 1 cheese

DIARY 3: Supper:

2 rolls, cheese dish, 1 Kit-Kat, tea

DIARY 2: Binge:

I began at 4.00 and finished 7.30. Bread, sausages, cheese, Sugar Puffs, sweets, Bonbons, then a second one on Twiglets, Cheese Puffs, sweets and crisps.

DIARY 1: Remarks:

Not too bad a day. Gilly and Anna finished their O-Levels and came home. Daddy is not really speaking to me. I binged because I just felt obsessional. I dread my weight tomorrow.

DIARY 3: Remarks:

This morning I really broke down and sobbed my heart out to Mummy and Daddy. I have just given up hope of ever getting better. Mummy, I am sure, is the only person who can help me. I had a dreadful afternoon bingeing and I have no idea how much food I retained in me, but it feels a lot.

DIARY 2: Remarks:

I am disturbed by my weight. I so wanted to talk to Mummy but we hardly said a word to each other until after my binge. Oh! I do love her so much. I dread my weight tomorrow.

DIARY 1: It is now 11.30 and the extra laxatives are not having much effect. I have had 145 laxatives today. My stomach is bloated and full of wind. May I not have gained tomorrow. I am so scared and mentally torn inside.

Dear Jesus, please help me.

I dread my weight tomorrow.

DIARY 1, 2 & 3: I dread my weight tomorrow.

Section 10

TWENTY-FIRST BIRTHDAY

MAUREEN: On the morning of Catherine's twenty-first birthday I persuaded her to let me take two polaroid photographs of her.

Slide* of the real **CATHERINE** *should be shown here (available from Salamander Street). The first slide should be the front view of* **CATHERINE** *head and shoulders.*

MAUREEN: She had just been released from an entirely unsuccessful stay in hospital weighing little over three stone. She was incontinent and had lost all muscle control. I hoped to shock her into seeing how she really looked.

The second slide* of the real **CATHERINE** *should be shown here… the full body shot… back view.*

(Silence.)

MAUREEN: Remember, Catherine was twenty-one years old.

The slide is turned off.

MAUREEN: The one condition I made before agreeing to bring Catherine home, was that she handed over her responsibility for eating to me. I made no mention of weight target, my overwhelming desire was that she should increase her weight sufficiently to prevent her death.

Four weeks after this Catherine weighed five stone. It seemed like a miracle. She acquired a job looking after two adorable little girls – Christina, aged one year, and Sarah who was three. She loved it and became very attached to the children.

---

* The slides referred to in this scene may be available for use for performances of the play only. For details contact Salamander Street (info@salamanderstreet.com).

Section 11

SUICIDE ATTEMPTS

The cast enter creating the environment of a kitchen. Their bodies make the various items used in the scene, including an oven (and hob), fridge freezer, sink (with optional waste disposal unit), food processor and pedal bin.

ANNA: On Sunday the 6th February 1983, Catherine made her first suicide attempt. The day before had been such a lovely day. It was Mummy and Daddy's twenty-fifth wedding anniversary. Catherine and I spent the whole day cooking and arranging everything for a surprise party.

CATHERINE: Preparation.

ANNA: Fridge Freezer. *(She opens it, and holds the door open for* **CATHERINE***. The fridge makes the sound of a 1980s fridge when open!)*

CATHERINE: Milk, eggs, butter. *(Collecting these items from the open fridge.* **ANNA** *then closes the door…)*

ANNA: *(Getting a mimed bowl, sugar & flour for* **CATHERINE***.)* Bowl… flour… and sugar.

CATHERINE: Glug, glug. *(As she pours the milk into a bowl.)* Crack… crack… crack. *(As she cracks the eggs into the bowl.)*

ANNA: Into the mixer. *(The elaborate "human" food processor makes appropriate sounds and actions.)*

CATHERINE & ANNA: Into the oven. *(Looking at the waste.)* Rubbish!

CATHERINE: Egg box.

ANNA: Milk carton.

CATHERINE: Butter wrapper. *(The "human" pedal bin burps!)*

CATHERINE & ANNA: *(As though resenting the task.)* Washing up.

ANNA: I'll dry.

CATHERINE: I can't wait to see Mummy and Daddy's faces when they get back.

ANNA: It'll be brilliant!

OVEN: Ding!

CATHERINE & ANNA: Ready.

*(As **CATHERINE** gets the cake out of the oven the cast, as kitchen environment, transforms to become the guests at the party.)*

ALL: *(Looking at the cake.)* Oooh… Ahh!

CATHERINE: Cake for Mummy and Daddy's Wedding Anniversary.

JOHN: *(Offstage.)* Beep beep!

ANNA: Car horn!

ALL: *(Looking off and saying melodramatically.)* Here they come! Hide! *(They hide.)*

JOHN & MAUREEN: *(Entering.)* Enter!

ALL: Jump! *(They jump out of their hiding place.)* Surprise!

SIMON: Champagne. *(Elaborate, comic mime with appropriate vocal sound effect of popping a champagne bottle.)* A toast!

ALL: To John and Maureen! A toast to Catherine.

SIMON: The idea of this surprise party was all Catherine's and it was she who'd phoned or written to invite all the guests.

MAUREEN: Her eyes never left our faces as we saw all of our guests, old friends we hadn't seen for years.

JOHN: The party was a tremendous success.

ANNA: A perfect evening.

*(**CATHERINE** silently and suddenly exits.)*

JOHN: The following day Maureen and I had been invited out for a celebration dinner… but when we got back…

MAUREEN: Anna… what exactly happened?

ANNA: Catherine came downstairs to make herself a drink and she collapsed. We didn't know what she had done at first, then Simon realised and I telephoned the hospital. There was nothing else we could do.

*(**ANNA** exits distressed.)*

MAUREEN: I knew we shouldn't have gone out. We should have realised that after all the effort she put into last night she'd feel empty this morning – and when she stayed in bed this morning… we just shouldn't have gone out.

JOHN: Maureen… Don't blame yourself. It's not your fault.

MAUREEN: At half past ten that night the phone rang.

CATHERINE: It's me. The doctor has said I can leave. You've got to come and get me out.

MAUREEN: She's obviously changed her mind since this afternoon.

CATHERINE: Yes. She said that I've made an exceptional recovery.

MAUREEN: Are you sure, darling?

CATHERINE: Of course I'm sure. If you don't believe me I shall make my own way home.

MAUREEN: Catherine, stay there, we'll be there as soon as we can! Whilst we were at the hospital, the Doctor came up to John in a very agitated state making out that John had corroborated with her discharge.

JOHN: I remember her saying that Catherine had very nearly killed herself and if it wasn't for the swift action of Simon, while we were out 'celebrating', we wouldn't even have a daughter to take home.

MAUREEN: John was furious!

JOHN: We've been doing all we can to dissuade Catherine from leaving this hospital. We've said everything we could think of but it'd proved absolutely useless. It was Catherine who was demanding to be discharged!

MAUREEN: She came home with us and for some days afterwards, remained in bed, sleeping a great deal. John and I had planned a week's visit to the Holy Land to mark our twenty-fifth wedding anniversary, and we were undecided about whether to go or not.

JOHN: The family, including Catherine, insisted that we should, and at the last minute we decided to go ahead with it.

MAUREEN: Our trip to the Holy Land became a pilgrimage on Catherine's behalf.

*(**MAUREEN** and **JOHN** exit.)*

CATHERINE: *(Musical box music.)*

26 February 1983:

Without Mummy I am totally unable to cope.

I dread and fear Daddy's reaction, his fury, frustration and anger because of my inability to be away from Mummy.

I am so filled with pain that I don't feel like eating.

I am like a newborn infant but with more feeling, fear and loneliness. At night I binge to try and numb my pain and torture myself.

Anna is being a little hard on me. If only she could understand. Where are my scales? I am sure that Anna has taken them.

*(She approaches **ANNA** who is asleep and jogs her aggressively.)*

CATHERINE: Anna! Anna, wake up!

ANNA: What do you want?

CATHERINE: I want to know where you have put my scales.

ANNA: I haven't touched your stupid scales. What would I want with them?

CATHERINE: I need to know where my scales are. I know you hid them!

ANNA: Okay, so I did!

CATHERINE: You wouldn't dare do this if Mummy and Daddy were here. You've no right to touch them.

ANNA: You've no right to be in my room!

CATHERINE: Tell me where they are Anna!

(Grabbing her violently.) I need to see how much I weigh!

ANNA: You know how much you bloody weigh!

Your obsession is ruining all our lives! And what's more, I know that you've begun hoarding tablets again. What are you trying to do? You've got enough to kill you four times over.

CATHERINE: I don't know what you're talking about.

ANNA: Alright, if you won't admit it, I'll show you!

(She runs to **CATHERINE***'s room.)*

CATHERINE: *(Running to the case and clutching it.)* You don't understand. They are helping me to get better. You don't want me to go on like this forever, do you?

ANNA: Won't you ever face up to the truth!

CATHERINE: Go away! Leave me in peace. I know what I am doing.

ANNA: So that's why they had to put you in a psychiatric hospital, isn't it? *(Fighting to get the case.)* Give it to me!

(In the struggle the case is opened and a vast number of medical bottles fall out.)

CATHERINE: Get out! *(Pushes* **ANNA** *away with great strength.)*

ANNA: I can't stand you when you're like this!

I hate being your sister!

CATHERINE: You'll regret saying that, Anna… you'll regret it.

(Pause. Cast enter with heads down audibly murmuring "Mummy, don't leave me" etc., repeatedly quoting Catherine in Section 4.)

SIMON: Shortly after Mum and Dad went away, Jenny and I were at a party and Catherine telephoned us to tell us that she had taken another overdose.

(Supporting cast suddenly fall silent. A long pause.)

We raced home to see her but when we arrived she denied taking the tablets. I was infuriated.

(Musical box music fades in and continues until **CATHERINE** *falls to the ground.)*

CATHERINE: 27 February 1983:

(Becoming increasingly desperate.)

Without Mummy I am totally unable to cope.

My anorexia takes more of a hold on me when she's not here.
I need her to keep me as sane as I will ever be.

I am not normal. I am odd. I shall never be able to work again.
I shall just become a lonesome invalid living in her own world.
I am on a knife's edge. I am cut into pieces so small that I can
never put them together again. I am so choked, I just cannot
carry on. God, please take me!

*(Each person in the cast quietly describes in meticulous detail and gives a
visual presentation of the moments leading up to the second suicide attempt
as though they are* **CATHERINE**.

Meanwhile **CATHERINE** *takes the overdose.)*

CATHERINE: Our Father who art in heaven.

ALL: *(As* **CATHERINE** *falls to the ground.)* No!

(The cast adopt a pained freeze momentarily and then exit in "neutral".)

ANNA: This is the second time, Simon. I can't bear it.

SIMON: I wouldn't have coped on my own.

ANNA: She's ruining everything for all of us. How am I meant to
concentrate on my A-Levels with all of this going on. I'm so
far behind because I just can't concentrate. When is it going to
end?

SIMON: It isn't something that comes and goes, Anna… breaking
free from it is probably worse than coming off heroin.

ANNA: Then why won't they make her stay in hospital?
They've got her there now. Why don't they make her stay?

SIMON: There's no point unless she's got the will to recover.

ANNA: Sending her home isn't going to make her better, is it?
She's so manipulative, she twists all of us round her little finger.
Maybe it would be better if she did die.

SIMON: Anna!

ANNA: We're just not brave enough to let her do it.

SIMON: She's going to get better… something is bound to turn up. Mum and Dad are going to be devastated. We've got to be strong for them.

ANNA: What about me, Simon? Everyone imagines that I go through all of this without getting at all upset. Good old Anna. She's strong, she can cope… she'll make everyone else feel okay. Well I've had enough of it all. No one ever thinks about me and how I'm feeling. It's not fair Simon, it's just not fair.

SIMON: The next day Mum and Dad returned.

JOHN: *(Entering with* **MAUREEN***, to* **SIMON** *and* **ANNA***.)* Is everything all right? Simon, where's Catherine?

SIMON: She's back in hospital. She tried to take her life again.

ANNA: *(Desperately; she is sitting avoiding eye contact with* **MAUREEN***.)* I can't handle it any more, Mummy, I really can't. If Catherine comes back home again I promise you, I'll leave. I can't live here with her. She frightens me; she does, she frightens me! Can't you make her stay in hospital, Mummy? You've got to make her stay there!

MAUREEN: *(Trying to calm her.)* Anna… Anna… We'll do all we can… you know we'll do all we can.

ANNA: *(Looking directly at* **MAUREEN***.)*
Well this time, Mummy, it may not be enough!
(Moves and looks away.)
I've thought about it really hard. I don't want to be anywhere near here when she dies… and she will. She will die if she isn't forced to stay in hospital. You've got to make her stay there, you've just got to!

(Two **NURSES** *walk to* **CATHERINE** *and hold and restrain her.)*

SIMON: Wouldn't it be possible to section her… under the Mental Health Act?

Section 12

SECTION 26 OF THE MENTAL HEALTH ACT

CATHERINE: You can't do this to me! Daddy, I hate you. I won't co-operate with the hospital regime so it's not going to do you any good.

DR CLEGG: Catherine, it's no use arguing. We're all in agreement. The time has come to take the matter out of your hands. You have been sectioned for a period of one year from this date.

CATHERINE: Where's my mother? She won't agree to this!

DR CLEGG: She knows where you are but she won't be allowed to visit you until we are sure that you are responding to our treatment.

CATHERINE: You can't keep me here. You have no rights over me!

DR CLEGG: Hospital admission… Catherine Dunbar. Aged twenty-two.

CATHERINE: I will eat.

DR CLEGG: *(Aggressively.)* Feed… feed.

MAUREEN: It was the same old story. She was co-operating to get out and then starve herself again at home. There was no attempt to determine the underlying causes of her anorexia and to deal with them.

Anorexia nervosa represents an arrest of puberty, and, in severe cases, a reversion towards childhood, reflected in the appearance and attitudes of the individual. She gains satisfaction and security from the way in which she is able to suppress her hunger and control both her body weight and body shape.

Every aspect of anorexia needs to be treated, not just the weight problem. How to cook food without becoming frenetic, how to sit down and eat with other people and, most importantly, how to form relationships. It is vitally important to help the patient make plans for the future and to rebuild her self-esteem.

Whenever possible, but particularly in severe cases, the treatment should be carried out by a specialist team, in a specialised unit, able to provide twenty-four hour support and therapy. I thought these 'experts' knew what they were doing.

DR CLEGG: *(Aggressively.)* Feed… Feed…

CATHERINE: Bloated.

DR CLEGG: Discharged. Catherine has reached her target weight but will be seen once a week while she is under section. If she maintains her weight for three months, we will then consider releasing her.

*(***DR CLEGG*** exits.)*

MAUREEN: Soon afterwards Catherine found a job working as a nanny and became very fond of the family.

I visited her at the weekends and she talked to me very honestly. It was clear that the thought of being released and free of doctors preoccupied her totally. She confided that she was still taking laxatives. She trusted me implicitly. I was torn in two.

DR CLEGG: Now look, to help Catherine you're going to have to tell me all of this in front of her. At the moment I think she sees you as an ally who accepts her illness. We must show her how much you hate the anorexia but love her. That way you can separate your love for Catherine from her anorexia.

MAUREEN: She'd hate me! It may even make her want to kill herself.

I can't take that risk.

DR CLEGG: She's like a young child and young children never hate their parents for long because they are too dependent on them. I realise how difficult it is for you, but it is crucially important.

*(***CATHERINE*** enters.)*

Hello, Catherine, how are you this week?

CATHERINE: I'm fine. I feel great. I'm really happy. My job is going perfectly and the children are so lovely. I really like it there. It's making me feel so much better.

DR CLEGG: Catherine… are you always being totally honest with me when you come here?

CATHERINE: What do you mean? I'm almost better.
I've got my problems haven't I? But who hasn't?
I **am** getting better.

DR CLEGG: I don't think that's true – is it, Catherine?

(Silence.)

MAUREEN: It's not… is it, Catherine? You're pretending because you're frightened that you'll be put back in hospital.

CATHERINE: I had a bad patch on Wednesday… but nothing serious. I have been eating… the only thing that's depressing me is the pressure of being sectioned. I know I'll be better when I'm off it.

MAUREEN: Catherine, you yourself have told me that the only way you feel you can be free of anorexia is to die.
*(To **DOCTOR**, crying.)* I just don't know what to say to her when she's like that.

DR CLEGG: Well, Catherine, from what your mother is saying it seems as though you're finding life quite difficult at the moment. *(Pause.)*

MAUREEN: Dr Clegg, there's another thing. Catherine is still taking laxatives… I'm sorry, Catherine, but I've got to be honest.

DR CLEGG: Do you understand why your mother is saying this, Catherine?

CATHERINE: *(Leaping to her feet and rushing out.)* You have no intention of releasing me from section – I hate you!!!

*(**MAUREEN** makes to go after **CATHERINE**.)*

DR CLEGG: No, don't! She's probably only gone to the car, she's not strong enough to go any further.

MAUREEN: As it turned out she'd made her way home where I was greeted by…

CATHERINE: Mummy!

*(As **MAUREEN** turns **CATHERINE** slaps her face hard.)* You betrayed me. I hate you! Why? You were the only person I ever trusted and you betrayed me.

MAUREEN: Catherine, can't you see that I betrayed your anorexia not you. I love you, I always have done. I loathe and hate your anorexia.

CATHERINE: It's who I am. Anorexia is a part of me and if you don't love my anorexia you don't love me.

(Silence… cries.) You don't understand!

(Pulls out chocolates and biscuits and throws them on the floor. Speaking calmly.)

I hate these chocolates, I never eat them. I don't even know why I take them. I just find them in my bag when I leave the shop. Afterwards

I feel awful, I hate myself.

MAUREEN: Catherine, you know what you have become… a common thief.

CATHERINE: Yes, I know… and I hate myself for it.

Do you know why I stopped eating so suddenly at the beginning?

MAUREEN: No… no… I'll never be sure of that.

CATHERINE: It was to protect you.

MAUREEN: Me?

CATHERINE: You see… I was frightened about you being alone with Daddy. The only way I'd be allowed home from school was to become ill, and the easiest way I could make myself ill was to stop eating. I did it to protect you.

*(**CATHERINE** exits.)*

Section 13

CATHERINE'S FINAL MONTHS

MAUREEN: Once free of the sectioning Catherine was more relaxed than I'd seen her for a long time.

JOHN: She started a new job in the middle of July 1983. She weighed seven and a half stone.

MAUREEN: Three months later she weighed only four stone four pounds.

JOHN: She returned home from work drained and exhausted. Finally, she was brought home by a social worker.

MAUREEN: She had come home to die.

SIMON: She prepared us individually for her death. She did not want us to mourn and insisted that we be happy for her as her suffering would have ended.

MAUREEN: I drove her to the little seaside town on the east coast where my mother had lived for so long, and where she had spent many happy childhood holidays. We visited the old haunts and it saddened me to realise that she was saying goodbye to them all. During her final weeks Catherine suffered intolerable physical pain. I wanted to envelop her in love… to demonstrate such love that she would not want to leave us. Her final outing was in a wheelchair to have her hair cut and to do her Christmas shopping. *(The sound of Christmas carols fade in. Perhaps this could be the same as that used in Section 2.)* Pushing her through the shopping precinct I could hear her singing along with Christmas carols being relayed over the loudspeaker.

ANNA: She was so looking forward to Christmas. 'Will you make sure everyone is happy over Christmas, Anna?' she said. 'I want it to be just like when I was a little girl.' She couldn't help me decorate the Christmas tree, so we carried her downstairs to see it. She thought it was the most beautiful tree that she'd seen.

Despite the sadness in all our hearts we attempted to make this Christmas a truly happy one for Catherine.

(The slide* of Catherine at Christmas in her final weeks can be shown here.)

We placed a bed in the drawing room so that she would be in the midst of the activity and when it was time for dinner we carried her, bed and all, into the dining room where she insisted that Mum should give her a normal portion of turkey, vegetables and trimmings. She attempted to chew the food, but deposited it in a basin.

MAUREEN: That night when I had settled her comfortably she said, 'This has been such a lovely day, please thank everyone for making it so happy.' The week following was one of quiet despair for us all.

(Pause.)

The 2nd January was to be the last day of her life.

At about 2:30 in the afternoon she indicated to me that she wanted a bath. Anna and I carried her to the bathroom.

ANNA: I supported her while Mummy washed her. At one point I changed the way I was holding her and her head hit the side of the bath; I was concerned in case she was hurt so, I asked her if she was all right. She just nodded. She gave me the impression that she didn't know where she was.

Looking back on it, I now realise that she had probably gone blind and didn't want to tell us that she couldn't see.

Afterwards I talc'd her. I wanted to make her smell lovely and refreshed. I wanted to show her how much I cared. We dressed her in her brand-new nightie. I told her how pretty she looked as I brushed her hair. She slept deeply all afternoon.

---

* The slide referred to in this scene may be available for use for performances of the play only. For details contact Salamander Street (info@salamanderstreet.com).

MAUREEN: Catherine died at 6:55 pm. She died at peace with God, with herself and with a heart full of love.

(Verse 3 of Away in a Manger.)

CHOIRBOY/GIRL: *(Unaccompanied.)*

Be near me Lord Jesus I ask thee to stay

Close by me forever

And love me I pray.

Bless all the dear children in thy tender care

And fit us forever

To live with thee there.

Section 14

THE BILLY GOATS – A NOTE OF OPTIMISM

NARRATOR: Once upon a time, there was a family of goats.

DADDY: There was a daddy goat.

MUMMY: There was a mummy goat.

BABY: And a baby goat.

ALL: Aaah!

MUMMY & DADDY: High expectations.

MUMMY: To cross the bridge.

DADDY: And to live in the green field.

MUMMY & DADDY: Just like we did when we were young.
    Cross the bridge.

BABY: But I must tidy my playpen.

MUMMY & DADDY: Cross the bridge.

BABY: Tidy my playpen.

MUMMY, DADDY & NARRATOR: *(Chanting.)*
    Cross the bridge… cross the bridge…
    cross the bridge… cross the bridge…

TROLL: *(Leaping onto the bridge, blocking* **BABY***'s path. Threatening.)* Troll!

BABY: Scared.

TROLL: *(Threatening.)* Troll!

BABY: Scared. *(Running to parents.)*

TROLL: *(Threatening.)* Troll!

MUMMY: Protection.

BABY: Safety.

DADDY: Seethe.

BABY: Playpen. *(Goes into it.)* Security.

DADDY: Open the door!

MUMMY: Leave Baby alone…

DADDY: Cross the bridge!

MUMMY: Be patient.

DADDY: Open the door.

MUMMY: Leave Baby alone.

DADDY: Cross the bridge!

MUMMY: Be patient.

DADDY: *(To **MUMMY**.)* Don't you see? Baby will never come out!

JOHN: In my view, no one or one event was totally to blame for Catherine's illness. It was the effect of her own physical and mental make up combined with the traumas and stresses of the family and the interactions of the individuals in it.

Looking back, I remember my strictness with the children, which probably made them nervous of me. I think of my rages and depressions during our family problems, which surely affected them deeply. I remember my lack of understanding that such a logical, intelligent girl could do this to herself; my sheer anger, intolerance and frustration which I used to voice to her in an attempt to shake her off this fatal course.

I tried logic, bribery, threats and pleaded with her even though it upset her. I had to keep on trying in the hope that any change of emotion, might arouse in her the desire and will to live.

All that I did or said was the best that I could do at that time, in those circumstances. My logical mind could not comprehend. Sadly, there is no logic in anorexia.

There will always be a deep feeling of extreme failure, sorrow and pain, for the loss of a lovely daughter with an illness which, it seems, no one understands.

I loved her dearly.

MAUREEN: I feel her loss so deeply. Her loss as a beautiful daughter, the loss of the children she might have had, my grandchildren, the loss of her, as a person. Who could have done and given so much. I hope I showed her and told her how much I loved her often enough.

To express my deepest feelings about Catherine's illness is impossible. Words fail me. Catherine and I underwent much pain and anguish together, but we enjoyed much that was good too. My hope always was that Catherine would overcome her anorexia and so, with her special knowledge, be able to help others, but she was trapped, trapped in a maze of agony and delusions.

There was one girl, however, who she was able to help. Patricia was a young girl, who was herself suffering from anorexia. She phoned only a few weeks before Catherine's death and asked to visit Catherine.

NARRATOR: Visitor from a neighbouring field.

JO: Jo the Goat. *(To* **MUMMY.***)* Playpen.

MUMMY: Cross the bridge.

JO: Playpen… just like Baby's.

MUMMY: Here it is… but our baby never came out.

TROLL: You can have one too. I'll build one for you…
You can have one too. I'll build one for you.

PATRICIA: When I first met Catherine, the sight of her shocked me so much it just blew my mind. I had never seen anything quite like it, but she was fantastic. She had been down that road before and really understood. She was determined for me to go into hospital and get well again. She really gave me strength. On the day that she died, I went up to the house and saw that her bedroom light was off.
Catherine's mother answered the door and I knew straight away. I stayed in her arms and she explained everything to me, most of all that Catherine was at peace now, rid of the devil that lived inside her. It made me kill the devil that lived in me

because it had killed the best friend that I could ever have.

MUMMY, DADDY, NARRATOR & JO: Cross the bridge… cross the bridge… cross the bridge…

TROLL: *(Disheartened.)*

You can have one too. I'll build one for you.

*(The **TROLL** sits on the bridge sobbing as **JO** successfully crosses the bridge.)*

ALL: Cross**ed** the bridge.

(Silence as the lights fade slowly.)

CROSSING THE BRIDGE

THE UNSEEN BILLY GOATS SCENES
c. 1988/2017

Introduction by Mark Wheeller

On the 10th March 1988 some of the younger members of my Oaklands Youth Theatre (OYT) made a hugely significant invention for *Hard to Swallow*. It would offer a way for me to include the optimistic ending to the play I had been looking for!

From my diary:

> **13/3/88**
> **On Thursday Debbie, Sharon, Chris and Richard came up with a brilliant Billy Goat story – "The Grass Is Always Greener on the Other Side". It was beautiful, simple and so appropriate.**

This story wasn't the short scenes that you will probably know that bookends the play which was to become *Hard to Swallow*. This scene was the germ that *led* to the idea.

While I was researching my book *Hard to Swallow – Easy to Digest[1]*, I discovered five Billy Goats scenes and a partially written performance poem. These were interpolated into the script, as it was at that time, to mirror or foreshadow key events in Catherine's story.

Until 2017, they had only been presented privately in our unseen rehearsals. I have decided to make them available as *Hard to Swallow* is increasingly being used as a study text in schools and I feel that these early prototype scenes shed some light on the meaning of the scene in the play.

Here, for the first time, they appear as part of the published playtext.

They also feature, as performed by my Romsey School Community Youth Theatre (RSCoYT), as a bonus feature on the *Hard to Swallow* DVD (2017).

---

[1] Available from Salamander Street.

These scenes will offer teachers using *Hard to Swallow* a unique way of introducing the Billy Goats to their classes, using a lesson or two to stage these little scenes imaginatively. The two scenes that appear in the final play will make so much more sense after working on these, not to mention the development of an appropriate physicalised performance style for them that can also feed into the rest of the play.

Teachers, directors and students often contact me asking:

'Why did you include Billy Goats?'

Some even dare to ask if they can cut them! Cut them??? Noooo!

I don't know how the idea originated. I love children's stories having a fresh spin on them and this one linked well to the idea of an anorexic regressing to childhood. More importantly, and on a practical level, I felt it was crucial for the play to have an attention-grabbing opening. A scene about Billy Goats would certainly not be what an audience would expect from a play about anorexia and the surprise would, I hoped, make the audience focus more intently. I wanted to throw our audience off balance!

Once it was in our minds to include such a story, we went to town. There were fifteen handwritten pages (about thirty minutes) of Billy Goats scenes in the original performance draft of the script. I remember thinking, when I looked at them for the first time in thirty years that some of them were surprisingly beautiful!

Once it was in our minds to include such a story, we went to town.

When I looked at the original draft of the play for the first time in thirty years I discovered there were fifteen handwritten pages (about thirty minutes) of Billy Goats scenes. I remember thinking they were surprisingly beautiful!

It is interesting to note that these original scenes refer to the field at the other side of the bridge as "enchanted" and having "beautiful flowers". At one point, Baby brings home sparkling rocks in an attempt to make his feuding parents happier.

We made Baby male, to show anorexia is not a female preserve.

The Troll's rhyme had a food related twist (I have no idea why we ditched it):

"I am the Troll and this is my bridge. If you dare to pass you'll be in my fridge!"

The playpen was originally a "tiny maze", built by Baby to take his mind off the dangers of the ugly (the reference here to the importance of appearance was not accidental) Troll. Baby was contented in it because, unlike other mazes, he had mastered this one and could never get lost in it. The maze was, over time, protected by an increasing number of doors Baby erects, preventing others from gaining access.

In the week of the first *Hard to Swallow* performances we did a run through and discovered the play was far too long. We were all thinking 'What do we cut?'. This wasn't a simple matter of cutting lines. It also meant we would have to cut roles. We needed to shed about thirty minutes.

"Right… Chris, Sharon etc. Go into the theatre while we look
at the main body of the play. Can you work on reducing the Billy Goats scenes
to one single scene lasting about five minutes!"

I don't remember any arguments. They just went and, using the same technique we used to reduce the ritual of Catherine visiting the hospital repeatedly over a few years, into a few minutes (what I call Précis [or Two Touch]). This small group of Year 9s cut the Billy Goats into pretty much the scenes that appear in *Hard to Swallow* today.

I didn't worry that it had lost a lot of the "beauty", something had to give! It had solved our problem fast and proved, even in this early presentation, entertaining. The group had been clever and we let them know how glad we were that they'd rescued us!

We knew this would make a great beginning to the play and then, if we reprised the scene at the end it would be… and then I thought if we mixed Patricia into it… oooh and John… oooh and Maureen. Wow!

That is how it came to be. No grand master plan. One idea led to another organically!

The Billy Goats are so important in this telling of Maureen's story. They:

- establish the style of performance with the Narrative/Précis Theatre and imaginative staging;

- offer a rare opportunity for liveliness and comedy;
- put the audience off balance by starting the play with unexpected content;
- are initially incomprehensible but by the end of the play, when the scene is reprised (in true TiE style), the audience become aware of what they have learnt because now the story, in the light of the *whole* story, makes complete sense;
- enables the play to end with a positive and upbeat message of hope.

So… please, please don't cut the Billy Goats but see them as an opportunity for all the above![2]

---

[2] These scenes, as performed by Mark's old Youth Theatre group, Romsey School Community Youth Theatre (RSCoYT), are available as a bonus feature on the *Hard to Swallow DVD* (2017) and can be downloaded from Salamander Street.

BILLY GOATS 1

Based on improvisations of Oaklands Youth Theatre 1988

Introduction

I think this must have been written to become the first scene of *Hard to Swallow* (at that point it was called "Catherine").

It establishes the Billy Goats family and sets up an outline of the outwardly perfect family with the nightmare, serving to foreshadow what is to come. Sometimes, things are not as perfect as they seem.

I think this was developed in a rehearsal by some of the cast. It seems that I liked and kept their opening but decided not to significantly develop the remainder of their scene.

In 2017 when the six goat scenes were performed by RSCoYT I realised the scene was too long, so, for this publication, I have edited it to make it a faster introduction.

It was the only scene, I felt, that still had problems in isolation.

Characters

Daddy Goat

Mummy Goat

Baby

Narrator

NARRATOR: Once upon a time, there was a family of Billy Goats. There was a Daddy Goat, a Mummy Goat and Baby Goat. They all seemed very happy. When Baby was born, Mummy and Daddy tethered him to a post in their field.

MUMMY & DADDY: We don't want Baby to stray too far away.

MUMMY: We want to be sure that he is safe…

MUMMY & DADDY: … and sound.

NARRATOR: Once tethered, Mummy and Daddy felt able to sleep more soundly…

MUMMY & DADDY: … more contentedly…

NARRATOR: … but

MUMMY, DADDY & NARRATOR: They had a terrible nightmare!

NARRATOR: Baby had grown up…

MUMMY: It's about time we let Baby have more rope, so he can go farther from home.

DADDY: Yes. We'll give him just enough to get to Farmer Jimbob's field.

NARRATOR: So, Daddy added more rope to Baby's tether.

BABY: Wonderful! I can run all the way to the Farmer Jimbob's field!

NARRATOR: And that's exactly what Baby did!

BABY: Hey there… can you see me?

NARRATOR: But no one heard Baby's words. No one was listening. When Baby returned, he was sad to see Mummy and Daddy bleating at each other… loudly.

MUMMY: What are you doing home? We thought you were far away!

BABY: I saw some beautiful flowers. I just had to pick them for you both!

MUMMY: Baby, these are beautiful. Thank you. That's really kind. Would you like to stay for tea?

BABY: I'd love to.

NARRATOR: So, they gathered as a family and had a civilised afternoon tea.

After a few days, the flowers began to wilt and Daddy said:

DADDY: Baby… let me give you some extra rope? We want you to explore the enchanted country beyond Farmer Jimbob's farm.

NARRATOR: Baby set off on his way.

MUMMY: Good luck Baby… and don't forget to write.

NARRATOR: Baby was not away long enough to write any letters and anyway, Goat Mail was very unreliable.

Once again, he returned and saw Mummy and Daddy not only bleating noisily at one another but lifting their hooves at one another.

MUMMY: What are you doing home? You should be far away!

BABY: I know, Mummy but, after I'd travelled beyond Farmer Jimbob's field, and through the enchanted country, I scaled the jagged mountain and saw these wonderful, sparkling rocks. I just had to bring one home to you.

MUMMY: Baby, these are beautiful. Thank you. Would you like to stay for tea?

BABY: I'd love to.

NARRATOR: So, they gathered as a family and had a civilised afternoon tea, but, after a few days, the sparkle from the rocks faded, leaving a rather dull and ordinary looking stone. So, Daddy said:

DADDY: I will give you all the rope I own so you can explore beyond the jagged mountain.

MUMMY: Good luck, Baby…. Don't forget to write.

NARRATOR: Many days passed.

MUMMY & DADDY: No letters arrived.

NARRATOR: There had been no postal strikes, so Mummy and Daddy assumed something might have happened.

They pulled in the rope but, to their dismay, attached to the end of the rope was not their Baby but the most precious, shimmering pearl from the ocean which lay beneath the jagged mountain.

They realised Baby was no more.
As suddenly as their nightmare had begun… it was over.
They rushed outside to see Baby, who was snoring heartily.
He was as safe as safe can be.

Once upon a time, there was a family of Billy Goats. There was a Daddy Goat, a Mummy Goat and Baby Goat. They all seemed…

FAMILY: … they all seemed…

FAMILY & NARRATOR:… very, very happy.

BILLY GOATS 2

Based on improvisations of Oaklands Youth Theatre 1988

Introduction

This scene happens towards what is now Section 4. It appears after the family have suffered their first (few?) first experience(s) of anorexia. John is just about to move to Saudi Arabia. It followed these lines which were eventually edited out and obviously indicate the "green field".

MAUREEN: It was about this time Catherine expressed a wish to…

CATHERINE: … go to school in France. I'd really enjoy it and it would give me a fresh start.

MAUREEN: I think it sounds like a wonderful idea.

CATHERINE: It'll help me to get better… I know it will.

MAUREEN: We'll have to convince the professor of that.
He didn't entirely approve but I felt that a complete change and challenge of her own making could only do her good. Through the convent she was attending it was arranged for her to transfer to their Mother House in Amiens.

DAD: We drove her to France just before I left for the Middle East.

This following short scene was developed by some of the cast. I made no changes.

The Troll appears for the first time and is defeated! I guess this is the hope the parents had that the change of environment would provide a simple solution that, sadly, it failed to do. It also includes the Troll's little rhyme which I think, maybe, I should have kept for the final play!

Characters

Daddy Goat

Mummy Goat

Baby

Troll

Narrator

NARRATOR: Once upon a time, there was a family of goats. There was Daddy Goat, Mummy Goat and Baby. They lived alone in Farmer Jimbob's field but had been there for so long that the field was almost bare.

One day Baby turned to his mummy and said:

BABY: Why don't we go and live in the enchanted country beyond Farmer Jimbob's field? The grass is much greener there and all our problems would be solved.

MUMMY: No. This is our home.

NARRATOR: But, by this time Baby was so desperate for the enchanted fields that…

DADDY: He decided to go alone.

MUMMY: … and came face to face

NARRATOR, MUMMY & DADDY: with the Troll. *(Ensemble repeat "Troll".)*

TROLL: I am the Troll. This is my bridge. If you dare to pass you'll be in my fridge!

BABY: Oh no!!! Let me cross. Mummy will soon follow. She's much tastier than me!

TROLL: Hmmm… okay… you may pass.

DADDY: Soon Mummy missed her child.

BABY: So, she decided to join him in the enchanted country!

MUMMY: … and came face to face

NARRATOR, MUMMY & DADDY: with the Troll. *(Ensemble repeat "Troll".)*

TROLL: I am the Troll. This is my bridge. If you dare to pass you'll be in my fridge!

DADDY: *(Pointing)* Look!

> **TROLL** *turns to look and* **DADDY** *kicks him off the bridge!*

NARRATOR: As the Troll fell to his doom, the bridge collapsed on top of him. He would never be seen again.

Once upon a time, there was a family of goats. There was Daddy Goat, Mummy Goat and Baby. They lived in alone, in a field in the enchanted country beyond Farmer Jimbob's field and stayed for a long time.

One day, Baby looked across to Farmer Jimbob's field and said:

BABY: Why does the grass always look greener on the other side?

BILLY GOATS 3
(Withdrawing from Society)

Based on improvisations of Oaklands Youth Theatre 1988

Introduction

This scene would interrupt what is now the end of Section 6 – the lines:

VOICE 4: Catherine…

ALL: … would you like to come out for a meal?

The plan was that the interrupted scene would have concluded at the end of the goat scene… possibly (though not in the version I have here) with the above line being repeated to remind the audience of the context. There were a couple of extra lines included in the after-words that ended up being cut.

VOICE 4: Catherine…

ALL: … would you like to come out for a meal?

MAUREEN: Catherine used to live in dread at being asked to the fortnightly dinners the other girls at the dental surgery liked to organise. She would feel guilty if she refused the invitation, as she believed the others would consider her unfriendly and aloof.

CATHERINE: Last night I felt such an oddity that I had to get a taxi at nine o'clock. I don't know how I'll face them at work on Monday.

MAUREEN: Despite the kindness of the young people, she would feel totally isolated.

In brackets at the top of this scene someone had written *(Withdrawing from Society)*.

The scene introduces the "maze" (later appearing in *Hard to Swallow* as a playpen.) The maze is a nice idea, as it is difficult to complete and would require determination to do so. The playpen more simply represents security.

This was developed by some of the cast. I had a hand in this, editing and developing the original improvisation and adding my own ideas.

<u>Characters</u>

Daddy Goat

Mummy Goat

Baby Goat

Friend

Troll

Narrator

Maureen

Catherine

NARRATOR: Once upon a time, there was a family of goats. There was Daddy Goat, Mummy Goat and Baby. They lived in alone Farmer Jimbob's field.

Baby built a little maze to play in. It would also protect him from the dangers he had heard about the Troll.

Baby had mastered his maze. He knew it back to front, and was so good that he had nearly forgotten why he had made it. He had completely forgotten about the Troll.

DADDY: Well done, Baby. We're really proud of you.

MUMMY: Yes. You're such a clever Baby!

GOAT FRIEND: Congratulations. Now, why don't you come across and try out the maze I built in my field?

BABY: Your maze looks really big and complicated. But… I'm so good at my maze that I think I shall try!

NARRATOR: So, with his new friend, Baby stepped into the big maze. At first, he was really confident but further on, he suddenly remembered the Troll. He became anxious that it might leap out and kill him!

BABY: I don't like this. I want to go back to my own maze. I know that one. I feel much safer in there.

NARRATOR: So, Baby returned to his own maze and stayed there for ever knowing the Troll could never get in and hurt him.

Once upon a time there was a family of goats. There was Daddy Goat, Mummy Goat and Baby. They lived in Farmer Jimbob's field. One day Baby said:

BABY: How is it you're not scared of the Troll?

BILLY GOATS 4

Based on improvisations of Oaklands Youth Theatre 1988

Introduction

This scene was planned to occur between Section 10 (Twenty-first birthday) and 11 (Suicide attempts).

The scene highlights Catherine's desperation and foreshadows the suicide attempts in the following section.

This scene was written by me. We were either running out of time or I was not satisfied with what the cast had managed to create.

The scene starts to question our reaction when confronted by a complex condition like anorexia. How much should we intervene?

The version the RSCoYT group have presented on the *Hard to Swallow* DVD is wonderfully imaginative and a great lesson in how to make a silk purse out of a sow's ear! (This isn't my greatest script.)

Characters

Mummy Goat

Daddy Goat

Baby

Troll

Narrator

NARRATOR: Once upon a time there was a family of goats. There was Daddy Goat, Mummy Goat and Baby. They lived in alone Farmer Jimbob's field.

Baby was spending more time playing on his own in his maze. Whenever he emerged he looked everywhere to check that he was safe from the Troll. One particularly sunny day Baby saw a beautiful bed of flowers in full bloom…

BABY: I must pick some of these to take home to Mummy and give her a surprise.

MUMMY: Oh Baby! They are so lovely. How sweet. Isn't that kind of him, Daddy?

DADDY: It is. Shall I put the kettle on a make a cup of tea?

MUMMY: That would be lovely!

BABY: I'll drink mine in my maze.

NARRATOR: So, Baby rushed off. Daddy switched the kettle on to make a cup of tea. When Baby arrived at the door to his maze he could not believe his eyes! There before him stood the Troll.

TROLL: I warned you I'd be back and here I am!

BABY: What do you want with me?

TROLL: I want to eat you up! Every bit of you.

NARRATOR: And with that Baby fled over the distant hill…

ALL: Chased by the Troll!

NARRATOR: Up the jagged mountain.

ALL: Chased by the Troll!

NARRATOR: He came to the mountain ledge that looked over the translucent ocean.

TROLL: The Troll stopped running.

NARRATOR: He knew that once in the translucent ocean Baby would be out of reach.

BABY: Troll? Why do you chase me? I don't mean you any harm.

NARRATOR: The Troll still climbed the mountain, licking his lips with his hairy tongue and rubbing his belly with glee.

TROLL: I curse you, Baby.

NARRATOR: Petrified, Baby took two steps forward on the thin mountain ledge and strained to see…

BABY: So… this… this is the translucent ocean everyone raves about. It looks…

NARRATOR: Back in Farmer Jimbob's field the kettle had boiled…

DADDY: Baby? Cup of tea!

NARRATOR: But Baby did not reply.

DADDY: Baby?

NARRATOR: Baby was not there.

DADDY: Baby? Cup of tea?

NARRATOR: Daddy went to see if…

DADDY: Mummy! Come quickly. Baby's not here…

MUM & DAD: … and the door to his maze is closed.

NARRATOR: They looked everywhere they could think of.

MUMMY: Hours passed.

DADDY: Night began to fall.

NARRATOR: They had lost hope.
Suddenly… they heard a distant bleating, the sound of…

DADDY: It's Baby!

MUMMY: Yes! I heard him too!

MUM & DAD: It's Baby!

NARRATOR: They looked to where the sound had come from and there, silhouetted against the night time sky, was the figure of a young goat straining to see over the edge of the jagged mountain.

They dared not make a sound for fear that… so… instead… they each made a wish that…

NARRATOR/MUMMY/DADDY: … time should stand still.

NARRATOR: Once upon a time there was a family of goats. There was Daddy Goat, Mummy Goat and Baby. They thought they lived alone in Farmer Jimbob's field but they knew that there had also been someone else.

TROLL: I curse you, Baby.

NARRATOR: If only Baby would come down from the mountain. But he never did. Lurking nearby, there would always be the flickering image of a Troll and deep down below, the translucent ocean looking so…

NARRATTOR/BABY: … so inviting.

BILLY GOATS 5

Based on improvisations of Oaklands Youth Theatre 1988

Introduction

This scene was planned to occur at the end of the play. At the time this was written the idea of amalgamating the stories and incorporating words from Maureen, John and Patricia had not come about. That resolved the problem of this being a good scene but lacking in power which those authentic words bring to it.

This was developed by the cast through improvisation and is clearly referenced in the Billy Goats story we chose to tell in the final version of *Hard to Swallow*.

The version that one RSCoYT group have presented is a fascinating interpretation and makes full use of the horror genre and was (amazingly), they tell me, inspired by Artaud's Theatre of Cruelty. They wanted to assault the audience's senses. I know the other RSCoYT members, when they first watched this, felt truly assaulted… and they loved it!

Characters

Mummy Goat

Baby

Jo the Goat

(Daddy Goat – may appear, according to interpretation, but has no lines)

Troll

NARRATOR: Once upon a time, there was a family of goats. There was Daddy Goat, Mummy Goat and Baby. They lived alone in Farmer Jimbob's field.

Baby had built a little maze to live in to protect him from the Troll. Now Baby had locked the door to the outside world.

One day, a goat from a neighbouring field came to visit, she was called…

NARRATOR/JO: …Jo the Goat.

MUMMY: Are you okay? Can I help?

JO: I've come to ask if I can see Baby? I've heard he's built a fantastic maze and I'm trying to build my own.

MUMMY: I can take you to the front door, but if you wish to see any further, you will have to ask Baby.

NARRATOR: So, Jo the Goat went to the door and knocked three times.

BABY: Who is it?

NARRATOR: The voice seemed to sound a long, long way away.

JO: I'm Jo the Goat, from a neighbouring field.

BABY: What do you want?

JO: I want to complete your maze. I've heard it's fantastic and I want to build one of my own.

BABY: Come in if you wish. I'd be interested to talk to you.

NARRATOR: Jo the Goat opened the door and, to her surprise, found another smaller door behind it. Behind this was another, even smaller door. So, it went on until, finally, she reached the tiniest door she had ever seen.

JO: Why is this door locked?

BABY: I don't remember why I locked it but I threw the key away long ago. You can look through the window.

NARRATOR: Jo could hardly move her head but she dipped and saw, all hunched up in the centre of the maze, not a goat, but the flickering image of a tiny Troll.

BABY: You are also building a maze of your own?

JO: I thought it would be safer.

BABY: Turn back. Find your way along the big maze. It must be much better than this!

JO: Why are you still here?

BABY: As I said before; I threw away the key. It's too late for me now… but it's not too late for you.

JO: Baby, I'm scared.

BABY: Look at me! Do you want to end up like this? Return to your field. Knock down your maze and find someone to help you into the big one. I'm sorry but I'm tired. I must go to sleep and dream of all the 'could have beens'. Dreaming's not for you, Jo the Goat. Go, and do what you decide is best.

JO: Is there anything I can do to help?

BABY: Yes. When you leave, please close all the doors.

JO: So, Jo the Goat turned and left, closing each door as quietly as she could. When she arrived back in her field she thought of poor lonely Baby who seemed more Troll than goat. With that in mind, she went back and pulled down her maze.

BABY: Baby breathed his last breath. It seemed like a sigh of relief… but the Troll in him was angry.

NARRATOR: Once upon a time, there was a family of goats. There was a Daddy Goat and a Mummy Goat.
They often thought of Baby and lived their lives as well as they could but nothing gave them greater joy than to see Jo the Goat in the enchanted fields, singing and playing happily like they did when they were young and undisturbed by Trolls.

BILLY GOATS 6
– CARELESS SILENCE COSTS LIVES

A PERFORMANCE POEM BY MARK WHEELLER

Based on the sketch of a poem written in 1988

<u>Introduction</u>

The performance poem is far more flexible in its casting than the other scenes. It can be performed by any sized group. In many ways… the bigger the better! (Although that also becomes harder to organise). When we at RSCoYT worked on this, we set ourselves one rule and one freedom.

– Everyone (in this 14-strong group) has to be actively involved throughout. (Rule)
– Spoken Lines (or even sub-lines) are to be allocated to individuals, pairs or groups. (Freedom)

I have no idea as to the origin of this poem. I discovered it as an incomplete poem at the end of the script. I am not sure if I'd been doodling or what but immediately it suggested a debate that has raged repeatedly in my own head when dealing with or developing work based on these, very serious, issues.

COULD my work have the effect of suggesting or even encouraging the very route that is being flagged up as a danger?

In *Too Much Punch For Judy*, I remember being aware of the possibility, that one of the professional cast (who, unlike most of my Epping Youth Theatre cast, were drivers) could themselves become involved in a drink-driving incident. I never imagined that "Judy" (the real person dramatised in the play) herself would repeat the same offence on the same stretch of road!!! If speaking out about her accident failed to prevent "Judy" from doing this again, how could I expect anyone merely watching the play to be more affected?

I believe making these plays can and positively affect (most) people's behaviour. I am admittedly working on a hunch (based on how I react to such things) rather than any hard evidence from a detailed study. The whole premise of my personal and professional life is that discussing difficult situations openly, is the best way forward.

It used to be said, in the war, *Careless Talk Costs Lives*. The opposite is also true… *Careless Silence Costs Lives* too!

CARELESS SILENCE COSTS LIVES

A Performance Poem by Mark Wheeller

The Billy Goat parents woke up one day
To find their Baby had gone astray
They looked to the left, they looked to the right
But their little Baby was nowhere in sight

They looked to the green fields and the mountain slope
Mummy ran inside and grabbed her telescope
Then, sliding into focus, they saw Baby's silhouette
High on the magical mountain ledge, frightened and upset

Chasing behind, the Troll reached out his hand
Baby thought the Troll was scary… he didn't
understand…
So, Baby veered towards the edge…

What should the Billy Goats have done?

There was no more edge left…

What should they have done?

Not a millimetre…

What could they have done?

Baby peered into the enchanted ocean, inviting and calm
And felt fear melt inside him as the Troll stretched out
his arm…

Shout at him!
Make him come home?
Talk him down… make him…

But before they decided, time ran out…
And left Mummy and Daddy in no doubt…

Baby Goat was…
Baby Goat… over and out.

Careless Silence Costs Lives

The Troll meanwhile, turned and fled
He knew he'd be blamed and again saw red…

Goats, humans, they're really the same
Trolls appear. They're easy to blame
Skill up in building bridges…
Bossing crossing bridges to the green fields…
Cross the Bridge… Boss the bridge…
Don't ever stop talking… don't ever stop walking…
Ignore the Trolls… easier said than won…
and you can win…
Cross the bridge…
Boss the bridge…
Cross**ed** the bridge

Hunchback

A poem believed to have been written by Catherine Dunbar.

He earned his living all right,
Only he didn't like being alive
Ever since he was small, ever since he could remember,
Life had been a terrible burden to him.
He was afraid to go out, afraid of others,
Of the way they looked at him…
Oh no, they didn't do any harm… but they looked – and they
laughed.
It was this laugh that made him suffer,
He was a hunchback.

Every day it was like this;
"Oh look, darling" a mother would say to her child
"Look at that little Hunchback, isn't he funny!"
"Hunchback, Hunchback" a man would cry, he wasn't bad,
But just cruel and wanted to impress his mates,
"Hunchback, come here so that I can touch your hump and have
some good luck!"
And the little hunchback bent his head and ran away.

It was like that everyday,
It had been like that everyday for years…
Yet he felt no hate in his heart.
He just realised that, in order to live with others you had to be like
everybody else.
He was a Hunchback: no room for him.
"Hunchback, hunchback!" that's all he heard in his silence…
in his sleepless nights.
So he wanted to sleep, to sleep without hearing, to sleep and forget…
Hunchback… Hunchback
Of course it was only a 'news item'
And of course there was only one corpse,
… But … how many murderers?

Digital Resources for Teachers

There are a number of practical digital resources for teachers and students who are studying *Hard to Swallow* as a set text.

See the Salamander Street website for

Hard to Swallow – Easy to Digest Student Workbook

by Mark Wheeller and Karen Latto

A video recording of *Hard to Swallow* is also available for download – please see the *Hard to Swallow* page on www.salamanderstreet.com for further details.

Hard to Swallow DVD/Download

The DVD includes:

Two productions.

The Romsey School Production, directed by Allie Clarke in 2017.

Oaklands Youth Theatre's original production (1990), directed by Mark Wheeller, performed in a Lecture Theatre of a hospital in Houston, Texas. (Filmed on a low budget camcorder).

Bonus Features:

Conversation between Allie Clarke and Mark Wheeller

Performances by Mark's RSCoYT of the *Crossing the Bridge – 6 previously unseen Billy Goat scenes.*

In light of this recent announcement from BTEC this DVD/download will provide opportunities to study Wheellerplays:

'You'll be pleased to hear that we will allow Mark Wheeller's plays to be used in Component 1 of the Tech Award. If it has recordings of a professional, student or youth theatre production that you can access, you are free to select it for use in Component 1.' Paul Webster

Available from Salamander Street.

Hard to Swallow – Easy to Digest

By Mark Wheeller

Including a new scheme of work by Karen Latto

Hard To Swallow is one of the five set texts for the new Eduqas GCSE (9-1) Drama examination.

This book has been developed to answer every question a teacher or a student might have about how *Hard to Swallow* was instigated, developed and progressed.

"I am absolutely over the moon with this resource! It has everything needed to inform students (and myself) ready for their exam and I couldn't be more happy with it. I would say that all drama teachers teaching Hard To Swallow *with their GCSE students use this resource as it really is invaluable and has made me so much more confident to teach this new syllabus. Thank you for creating this resource."*
Nikki Law

Paperback 9781913630416
eBook 9781913630423

Available from Salamander Street and all good bookshops.

Teachers – if you are interested in buying a set of texts for your class please email info@salamanderstreet.com – we would be happy to discuss discounts and keep you up to date with our latest publications and study guides.

Salamander Street will be publishing new editions of Mark's plays in 2020 – follow us on Twitter or Facebook or visit our website for the latest news.